A2 Psychology
UNIT 4A

Clinical Psychology

Christine Brain

Philip Allan Updates
Market Place
Deddington
Oxfordshire
OX15 0SE

tel: 01869 338652
fax: 01869 337590
e-mail: sales@philipallan.co.uk
www.philipallan.co.uk

This Guide has been written specifically to support students preparing for the
Edexcel A2 Psychology Unit 4 examination. The content has been neither
approved nor endorsed by Edexcel and remains the sole responsibility of the
author.

Printed by Raithby, Lawrence & Co. Ltd, Leicester

Contents

Introduction

■ ■ ■

Content Guidance

■ ■ ■

Questions and Answers

Introduction

About this guide

This is a guide to Unit 4A of the Edexcel A2 specification: Clinical Psychology. Before looking at what this guide is all about, here is some good news (in the form of positive reinforcement). You can pass the exam for this unit, and you can do well. How can I draw this conclusion without knowing you? Because you are reading this guide.

Students who takes the trouble to read this sort of guide:
- are motivated to do well
- have an idea about where to look for help
- understand what unit they are taking, and with which examination board
- know something about active learning — we can learn better if we engage in tasks, such as using this sort of student guide

So you already have some of the skills and knowledge you need — hence my claim that you can do well. However, this guide:
- is not a textbook — there is no substitute for reading the required material and taking notes
- does not tell you the actual questions on your paper, or give you the answers!

Aims

The aim of this guide is to provide you with a clear understanding of the requirements of Unit 4A of the A2 specification and to advise you on how best to meet these requirements.

This guide will look at:
- the psychology you need to know about
- what you need to be able to do and what skills you need
- how you could go about learning the necessary material
- what is being examined
- what you should expect in the examination for this application
- how you could tackle the different styles of exam question
- the format of the exam, including what questions might look like
- how questions are marked, including examples of answers, with examiner's comments

How to use this guide

A good way to use this guide is to read it through in the order in which it is presented. Alternatively, you can consider each topic in the Content Guidance section, and then turn to the relevant question in the Question and Answer section.

Whichever way you use the guide, try some of the questions yourself to test your learning. Hopefully, you will know enough about the marking by this time to try to grade your own answers. If you are working with someone else, mark each other's answers.

The more you work on what is needed, the better. Have other textbooks available too — you will need access to all the relevant information.

Study skills and revision strategies

If you have been studying the Unit 4 material on Clinical Psychology, and have engaged in a reasonable amount of learning up to now, you can make good use of this guide.

This guide can also help if you know very little of the material and have only a short time before the examination. If this describes you, you have a lot of work and long hours of study ahead — but you can do it.

Before reading on, answer the following questions:
- How long is left before the exam?
- Do you have a revision plan?
- Are you sure you want to pass, and hopefully do well? Renewing your motivation can help.
- Are you stressed and in a panic?
- Can you stick to your plan, and trust it?

If you need to, draw up a revision plan now, remind yourself that you do want to succeed, and practise some relaxation techniques.

Revision plan
- Start at least 4 weeks before the exam date (sooner if possible).
- Using times that suit you (6 a.m. might be a great time to study!), draw up a blank timetable for each of the weeks.
- On the timetable, fill in all your urgent commitments (cancel as many plans as you can).
- Divide up what is left, allocating slots to all your subjects as appropriate. Don't forget to build in meal times, breaks and time for sleep.
- Stick to the plan if at all possible, but if you have to, amend it as you go.
- When studying, have frequent, short rests and no distractions.

Time management
Answer the following questions to see how good you are at time management.

(1) Are you usually punctual?
  yes   no

(2) Do you tend to work fast and then correct mistakes?

　　yes　　no

(3) Do you often put things off?

　　yes　　no

(4) Do you feel stressed because you never have enough time?

　　yes　　no

(5) Do you work slowly and carefully, and try to get things right first time?

　　yes　　no

(6) Do you daydream?

　　yes　　no

(7) Are you forgetful?

　　yes　　no

(8) Do you find it hard to get started?

　　yes　　no

(9) Do you keep your desk tidy?

　　yes　　no

Score 0 for 'yes' and 1 for 'no' to questions 1, 5 and 9. Score 1 for 'yes' and 0 for 'no' to questions 2, 3, 4, 6, 7 and 8. A score of 3 or below means your time management is quite good; a score of 4 and above means you need to work on it.

Relaxation techniques

Boxes 1, 2 and 3 suggest some ways to relax. Use these as appropriate.

Box 1: Technique 1 — takes about 10 minutes

This technique is useful at the start or end of a longish revision period.

- Lie on the floor and make yourself comfortable.

- Working from toes to head, tense each of your muscles in turn and then relax.

- Having relaxed your body, now relax your thoughts.

- Take yourself in your mind to a place where you feel at peace — this could be a favourite holiday place, or a favourite place on a walk. Closing your eyes will help.

- Have a good look around (mentally!), sit down there and listen to the sounds of the place.

- Stay there and try not to come back yet.

- When you are ready, come back. Slowly start to hear the sounds around you, and lie with your body relaxed for a little while longer.

Box 2: Technique 2 — takes about 5 minutes

This technique is useful as you revise. Work for between 30 minutes and an hour, and then stop to relax as follows:

- Sit comfortably and try to ignore anything going on around you.

- Imagine you are in a barn, sitting on the rafters under the roof, swinging your legs and sitting comfortably. Closing your eyes will help.

- Now, imagine that the barn has open doors at both ends, and there is a river rushing through from one end of the barn to the other. You are sitting swinging your legs, watching the river rush through below you.

- Hear the water rushing through, sit comfortably, and just watch.

- Think of the water as your thoughts rushing away.

- You are not involved, just watching.

- After about 3 minutes or when you are ready, slowly start to hear the sounds around you, and gradually bring your thoughts back into the real world. Look around you for a minute or two and check that you feel better, before getting back to work.

Box 3: Technique 3 — takes about 1 minute

This technique is useful when you are actually in the examination, and can be used if you are too anxious to continue.

- Imagine you are in an exam now.

- Imagine that you are getting anxious.

- Pick up a pen as if to write.

- Hold the pen up in front of you and stare at it.

- Let all your other thoughts go and think about the pen.

- Try to think of nothing else even for a few seconds.

- Get back to work!

Examination structure and skills

Unit 4 consists of five applications of psychology: clinical, criminological, education, work and sport. You must select *two* of these applications to study and you will have to answer questions on both of them in the exam.

There will be three questions for each application which may be divided into separate parts. Although there are three main areas to the specification for each application, there will not necessarily be one question for each of these areas. It is not possible to guess what is going to be on the paper — don't try. Prepare answers for all possible questions. If you know the material, read the questions carefully and do what is asked, you will do well.

Assessment objectives

The assessment objectives are listed in the specification. A brief explanation is given below, but check the full list of what you will be assessed on.

Assessment Objective 1: knowledge and understanding (AO1)
- You need to explain your knowledge and understanding of psychological terminology and concepts through appropriate use and application.
- You must demonstrate knowledge and understanding of psychological theories, studies, methods and concepts, as well as psychological principles, perspectives and applications.
- You must communicate clearly and effectively, and present and select material well.

Assessment Objective 2: evaluation and comment (AO2)
You must be able to:
- analyse and evaluate psychological theories and concepts, referring to relevant evidence
- appraise psychological studies and methods

Assessment Objective 3 (AO3)
Assessment Objective 3 is examined in Units 3 and 5, and is not dealt with here.

The Unit 4 exam

Unit 4 is assessed in a 90-minute exam. 72 marks are available — 36 for each application. This means you need to score around 1 mark per minute, with 18 minutes to spare for reading and thinking. In general, you can expect to gain 1 mark for each point that answers the question, or for elaboration of a point. Answers must be communicated 'clearly and effectively' (see AO1 above). Avoid one-word answers and bullet points unless they are asked for. Some Unit 4 papers require you to write an essay at the end of each question, and some do not. You should be prepared to write an essay worth between 12 and 16 marks. Overall, each application has approximately 15 marks for knowledge and understanding (AO1) and 21 marks for evaluation and comment (AO2).

Essay mark scheme
The essays have 2 marks (AO1 marks) available for clarity and communication (use of terms, spelling, ways of expressing points) and 2 marks (AO2 marks) for balance and breadth. In addition, for a 12-mark essay, you need to give four AO1 'knowledge and understanding' points and four AO2 'evaluation and comment' points. For a 14-mark essay, five AO1 points and five AO2 points are required. For a 16-mark essay, six AO1 points and six AO2 points are required.

AO1 and AO2: getting it right
You must be sure to answer the question that is set — you should then cover the AO1 and AO2 skills. The key words in the question (called **injunctions**) guide what you need to write. If you answer the question, you will automatically do what is required.

Table 1 shows some examples of how AO1 injunctions are used and Table 2 shows examples of AO2 injunctions. Note that it is not so much the word itself (e.g. 'describe') that makes it AO1 or AO2, as the whole question. The figures in brackets suggest the mark allocation you might expect for such a question.

Table 1 Examples of AO1 questions/injunctions

Type of question	What is being asked for
Describe a therapy... (4)	Say what something is (a therapy in this case). Imagine describing the therapy to someone who knows little about it.
Identify a therapy... (1)	Give enough information so that the examiner can understand what is being referred to. For example, if asked to identify a behaviourist therapy, write about the use of tokens as positive reinforcers.
Name a therapy... (1)	Name either the therapy or the psychologist(s). An example might be systematic desensitisation.
Outline a definition... (3)	Follow the instruction for describe, but remember that this injunction usually requires less detail, and hence carries fewer marks.
Describe a study... (5)	Try to give the aim of the study, the method, the procedure, the results and the conclusion(s).

Table 2 Examples of AO2 questions/injunctions

Type of question	What is being asked for
Outline a strength of... (2)	You are asked to outline something, so the injunction seems to be AO1 (i.e. knowledge and understanding). However, as what is outlined is a *strength* (in this case), and thus you are being asked to evaluate something, this question would carry AO2 marks. Note, though, that you must still 'outline' (see Table 1).
Evaluate a study... (5)	Give comments, criticisms, good points and so on about a study. Consider strengths and weaknesses of the method, perhaps, or criticisms of ethics involved. Look at alternative findings or consider whether justified conclusions are drawn.
Compare two therapeutic approaches... (6)	Give some information about one therapeutic approach (e.g. psychoanalysis) and say how it is different from or similar to another approach (e.g. the behaviourist approach).
Assess the effect of... (4)	Show what the effect of something is (e.g. use of a token economy programme) and then suggest to what extent this is useful (assess).

AO1 and AO2: injunctions in essay questions

Essay questions will always involve equal marks for AO1 and AO2. You should demonstrate knowledge and understanding and provide comment and evaluation. Remember spelling and use of terminology (2 AO1 marks for clarity and communication). Make sure you address all parts of the question (2 AO2 marks for breadth and balance).

Table 3 shows the importance of knowing how AO1 and AO2 marks are split in each examination paper (excluding Unit 3, the coursework element and Unit 5, which involves some AO3 marks).

Table 3 Approximate mark allocation AO1/AO2

	AO1	AO2	Total
AS Units 1 and 2	42	30	72
A2 Unit 4	28	44	72
A2 Unit 6	36	36	72

Table 3 shows how, for the two AS units, you were assessed more on your knowledge and understanding (58%) than on your ability to comment and evaluate (42%). For Unit 4, you will be assessed more on your ability to comment and evaluate (61%) than on your knowledge and understanding (39%). For Unit 6, your knowledge and understanding and your evaluation and comment skills are assessed equally.

Essentially, you have to learn the material so you know and understand it, and then plan some criticisms, comments and evaluation points. As a rule of thumb, learn or plan as many evaluation and comment points as you learn information points.

Conclusions: use of injunctions and AO1/AO2 split

Don't just think of a word in the question as being the whole question. For example, 'describe' is an AO1 command, but 'describe a strength...' is an AO2 injunction. 'Discuss' could signal AO2 marks if you are asked to 'discuss the usefulness of...' Because you are considering how useful something is, you are doing more than showing knowledge about it. The best approach is to *answer the question*. If you study and understand the question, all should be well.

Differences between AS and A2

Although a lot of what is true for AS applies to A2 — for example, the AO1 and AO2 assessment objectives — the A2 exams require higher-level skills. At A2, more marks are given for AO2 (evaluation and comment) than for AO1 (knowledge and understanding), except Unit 6 where both skills are assessed equally. This is quite different from AS. It means you need to comment, evaluate, assess, consider strengths, and so on, more than you need to give information. When you are making notes and preparing answers to exam questions, remember to concentrate on criticisms. Whenever you read an evaluation point, note it down and learn it.

Greater depth is also required in your answers at A2. For example, if you are asked to consider issues regarding the reliability of diagnosis, you need to be ready to give relevant evidence — and that tends to mean studies. The specification might not ask you expressly to learn studies that show that, for example, schizophrenia has a genetic cause (at least in part), but you will need to refer to relevant evidence to support your answers (AO2). Psychology is built on evidence from studies, so when revising it is useful to have a list of names of studies and a brief outline of what each is about.

Content Guidance

This section provides an overview of what you need to learn for Unit 4A. It includes some AO1 (knowledge and understanding) material for each topic, as well as AO2 evaluation points and is divided into the following topics:

Defining and classification

- Definitions of abnormality
- The *DSM* classification system

When looking at different definitions of abnormality, or problems with diagnosing mental illness, you will probably have covered very similar material to that given here. However, only two definitions of abnormality are required, so you may have studied different ones from those chosen.

Approaches and therapies

- The medical/biological approach
- The psychodynamic approach
- The behavioural approach
- The cognitive approach
- The humanistic approach
- The social approach
- Comparing the six approaches

You need to be able to compare these six approaches to mental disorders and consider similarities and differences between them. When looking at the six approaches and the way they deal with mental health issues, you will probably have covered very similar basic material to that presented in this guide. However, you may have looked at different examples of therapies.

Specific mental disorders

- schizophrenia
- mood disorders (including unipolar and bipolar)

When studying specific disorders, you need to look at symptoms and possible causes in terms of physiological, social and psychological factors. If you have studied the other two disorders on the specification (eating disorders and anxiety disorders), you need to decide whether to add to the material you must revise by including the two outlined here, or whether to keep to your own notes.

Defining and classification
Definitions of abnormality

Many terms have been used to represent the idea of mental illness. It is not an easy concept to define, but defining it is important for practical reasons to do with diagnosing a problem and suggesting a cause and/or cure.

> **Tip**
>
> You only need to learn two of the following definitions, but a third is useful for comparison and evaluation.

Abnormality as deviation from statistical norms

This definition suggests that anything infrequent is abnormal. Anybody whose behaviour differs from the norm (i.e. is outside the middle range called 'normal') is called 'abnormal'. This is not a good definition. People with very high IQ scores, for example, are not normal, but we would probably not say they were abnormal in the sense of being mentally ill.

> **Evaluation**
>
> + We can decide on a division to separate normal from abnormal. For example, an IQ score at the lower end (e.g. 70) could be the defining line between normal and abnormal. This means abnormality is easy to 'diagnose'.
> − Having a single cut-off point presents difficulties. Who decides where that line lies? For example, if 70 IQ points is the cut-off, how can we justify saying that someone with 69 is abnormal, and someone with 70 is normal?
> − One score may not be enough to define someone as abnormal. It may be necessary to look at more than one measure and not, for example, IQ alone.

Abnormality as deviation from social norms

This defines abnormality as unusual social behaviour. Someone might behave abnormally by showing strange, obsessive behaviour or violating social norms, such as wearing nightclothes in the street.

> **Evaluation**
>
> + We tend to think of abnormality as behaving oddly, so this definition has appeal.
> + Those with mental health problems do break social norms fairly often.
> − There may need to be several examples of antisocial behaviour before we are willing to label someone as 'abnormal' in the sense of mentally ill. Perhaps wearing night

clothes in the street and singing suggests abnormality more strongly than just wearing nightclothes, which you might do in an emergency.
- Criminals violate social norms but are not usually thought of as being mentally ill.
- Some people might be mentally ill, perhaps suffering from intense anxiety, but they might not break social norms.
- There are cultural differences in social norms, so measuring abnormality by means of such norms, which are not fixed, is unlikely to be useful.

Abnormality as dysfunction and distress

One way to define abnormality is to see if it is causing a problem for the person concerned. For example, people can have a fear of something yet only be diagnosed as having a phobia if that fear is preventing them from functioning in some way. If people cannot work because of their fear, then that is dysfunctional — it is interrupting their normal functioning and distressing them.

It could be that people function quite well by avoiding problem areas. For example, people may suffer from social phobia but not have a problem because they do not go out. However, this is still dysfunctional and would be thought of as a problem that needs treatment, so should be diagnosed.

Evaluation

+ This is quite easy to apply as it is usually obvious when something is causing a problem. For example, it is dysfunctional for people if they cannot go out or go to work.
- However, what one person thinks of as abnormal and dysfunctional, such as not going out, someone else might consider quite normal. There is an element of subjectivity in the judgement.
- Psychopaths may need diagnosing, but may not be suffering any distress, and may be functioning normally as far as others can see.
- It is hard to measure distress, as this is subjective and differs between individuals.

Summary

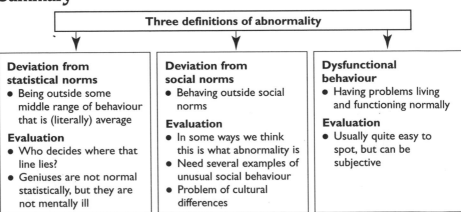

Three definitions of abnormality		
Deviation from statistical norms • Being outside some middle range of behaviour that is (literally) average **Evaluation** • Who decides where that line lies? • Geniuses are not normal statistically, but they are not mentally ill	**Deviation from social norms** • Behaving outside social norms **Evaluation** • In some ways we think this is what abnormality is • Need several examples of unusual social behaviour • Problem of cultural differences	**Dysfunctional behaviour** • Having problems living and functioning normally **Evaluation** • Usually quite easy to spot, but can be subjective

The *DSM* classification system

The *DSM* is the *Diagnostic and Statistical Manual of Mental Disorders* and is published by the American Psychological Association (APA). The most recent version is *DSM-IV*, which was published in 1994. There are other classification systems, but it is the *DSM* that you need to know about. Doctors use the *DSM* to diagnose mental illness. It contains lists of symptoms that the patient's symptoms are matched to, with the best match being the diagnosis.

DSM-IV looks at the pattern of symptoms, including the distress the person is experiencing. It uses a definition of abnormality linked to distress of the person and dysfunctioning; it is not just a list of physical symptoms. Someone simply behaving contrary to social norms would not be considered abnormal, and neither would someone who behaves abnormally 'statistically'.

DSM-IV is a multiaxial system, which means it looks at patterns across different dimensions. The five axes of *DSM-IV* are outlined in Table 1.

Table 1 **DSM-IV's five axes**

Axes and examples	Description
Axis I includes: • disorders usually first diagnosed in infancy, childhood or adolescence • substance-related disorders • schizophrenia/psychotic disorders • mood disorders • anxiety disorders • eating disorders	Any clinical disorder or conditions already present, other than personality disorders and mental retardation
Axis II includes: • personality disorders • other conditions (e.g. problems relating to abuse or neglect)	Personality disorders and mental retardation
Axis III includes: • general medical conditions	Other general medical conditions that may affect diagnosis
Axis IV includes: • problems with family • educational problems • housing problems • economic problems	Psychosocial and/or environmental problems that may affect diagnosis
Axis V includes: • psychological, social and occupational functioning along a continuum of mental illness to mental health (e.g. from 0–100 with 10 being in (persistent) danger of hurting themselves and 90 being minimal symptoms, such as anxiety before an exam)	Global Assessment of Functioning (GAF)

To diagnose, the clinician considers all five axes. Someone might be involved in substance abuse (Axis I), have a personality disorder (Axis II), have no other medical problems (Axis III), have educational problems (Axis IV) and be at risk of self-harm (Axis V). One of these would be the diagnosis, possibly the personality disorder. As you can see, having one problem is not enough for diagnosis, although in practice having a severe eating disorder, for example, is likely to lead to a low rating on the Global Assessment of Functioning scale (Axis V).

Another system, the *International Classification of Diseases* (*ICD*), is published by the World Health Organisation (WHO) and used across the world. *ICD-10* was published in 1993. However, DSM is used widely, partly because many books on clinical psychology and diagnosis are American in origin.

Evaluation

+ Costa and McCrae (1992) developed the Five-Factor Model of Personality (FFM) which considers neuroticism, agreeableness, conscientiousness, extroversion and openness to be the basic dimensions of personality. These dimensions have been used to diagnose personality disorders. It has been found that diagnoses based on the FFM have correlated with those using Axis II of the *DSM*, which gives it reliability.
+ The *DSM* has many specifics to try to ensure reliability and consistency. Reliability of diagnosis means that one person will receive the same diagnosis from different clinicians. Likewise, they will receive the same diagnosis if they go back to the same clinician at a different time with the same symptoms. Specific lists help to ensure reliability, but have their limitations (as discussed below).
+ Validity is also supported by having specific categories and examples in the manual. It is achieved when something measures what it claims to measure. In other words, if you are diagnosed as having schizophrenia, then that is the case, and treatments for schizophrenia will hopefully work. Validity is important because if you are diagnosed wrongly, you might receive the wrong treatment. *DSM-IV*, with its greater detail, is supposed to have improved reliability and validity.
− Categorising is a limiting process because mental illness does not fall into categories so much as being along a continuum. We do not tend to be mentally ill or mentally healthy, but somewhere in between. This can be the case on different days, in different places, on different occasions. Diagnosing is not as straightforward as putting people into categories, which is what a classification system does.
− What counts as an illness changes over time. For example, homosexuality used to be in the manual, whereas it is not now considered a mental illness. However, if homosexuality is affecting someone, in that perhaps they wish to change their sexuality, then it can be diagnosed under a heading such as 'sexual disorder not otherwise specified'.

Implications of diagnosis of mental health issues

Advantages of being diagnosed

It might be thought that there is nothing to be gained from being diagnosed (labelled) as having a particular mental illness (or group of illnesses). You may have studied labelling and the effect of a self-fulfilling prophecy, and seen how it can be detrimental to someone. However, there are advantages to having a 'label':

- Financial help can be given in the form of allowances and support.
- In theory, any treatment offered should be suitable. A wrong diagnosis is likely to lead to the wrong treatment.
- Research can be carried out more easily, as people will have been grouped by their diagnosis, so can be grouped for the purposes of study. This might yield more information about the cause of the disorder, or more ideas concerning treatments and therapies, which can be advantageous to the individual.

Summary

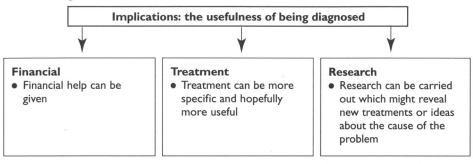

Diagnosis can be useful for the individual, but there are also disadvantages, which tend to concern validity, reliability and cultural factors.

Validity of diagnosis of mental health issues

If a diagnosis predicts the course of the illness and the symptoms, then it is useful. It is also useful if it leads to the right treatment and the treatment works. For these things to be true, the diagnosis must be valid — it must measure what it is supposed to measure and the classification system must lead to the diagnosis of the right illness.

Etiological validity

Etiological validity is found when a diagnosed problem is said to have the same cause for all those diagnosed with it. For example, if we say that bipolar disorder (manic depression) has a genetic cause, then all sufferers should have a history of it somewhere in their family.

Concurrent validity

Concurrent validity is when other symptoms or factors found in one person, but not seen as part of the diagnosis, are also found in others with the same diagnosis. An example might be if all those with schizophrenia were found to have problems relating to others (which is not itself part of the diagnosis).

Predictive validity

Predictive validity means that those with that diagnosis follow the same future path — the course of the illness is the same.

How can we tell if a diagnosis is valid?

Robins and Guze (1970) suggest that to see if a diagnosis is valid, we need to check that:

- the diagnosed illness fits in ways other than those based only on symptoms. For example, the person might be in some other suitable category in which this illness occurs often (e.g. gender or age group).
- the symptoms usually go together, and do in this case too
- the symptoms do not all occur in another illness
- the disorder tends to run in families, and that is true for this particular case

Evaluation

- There are problems with validity. For example, manic depression is difficult to diagnose and is often misdiagnosed as schizophrenia or depression in the first instance.
- Symptoms often apply to various illnesses, so problems with diagnosis can occur. For example, paranoia can represent schizophrenia or substance abuse.
- If it were the case that one symptom represented one illness, there would perhaps be few problems. However, people are different, and although each illness might have a recognisable pattern, it is often not exactly the same for each person, so predictive validity is in doubt.

Reliability of diagnosis of mental health issues

Reliability means that if something is done again, the same results are found. For example, if more than one psychologist gives the same diagnosis for the same set of symptoms (for the same person), then that diagnosis is considered reliable. If different psychiatrists do give the same diagnosis, this is inter-rater reliability. Reliability would also be found if the same psychologist, on being presented with the same set of symptoms (for the same person) on a different occasion, would again give the same diagnosis.

However, psychologists can give different diagnoses for the same set of symptoms (which means diagnosis is unreliable). If diagnosis is unreliable, then treatment is possibly going to be incorrect and not helpful. The treatment could be bad for the patient who might miss out on relief from more appropriate therapy. Beck et al. (1961) gave two psychiatrists the same 153 patients to diagnose and they only agreed 54% of the time. This suggests that diagnosis is not reliable. Meehl (1977), however, argued that if all the categories are considered, and information is complete, then diagnosis can be reliable.

Evaluation

- Unstructured interviews are not reliable and are often used.
- Sometimes all the information is not gathered.
- Some mental illnesses are hard to diagnose.
- Different diagnoses may reflect that psychiatrists can be subjective.

- Perhaps the misdiagnosis is deliberate because some institutions only admit those with certain problems and the psychiatrist wants a particular patient to be admitted.
- Cultural factors may affect reliability.

Summary

Validity and reliability of diagnosis of mental health issues	
Validity of diagnosis • If a diagnosis predicts the course of the illness and the symptoms, it is useful • It is also useful if it leads to the right treatment and the treatment works • The diagnosis must be valid — it must measure what it is supposed to measure • The classification system must lead to the diagnosis of the right illness	**Reliability of diagnosis** • Reliability means that if something is done again, the same results are found • If more than one psychologist gives the same diagnosis for the same set of symptoms (for the same person), then that diagnosis is considered reliable • Reliability would also be found if the same psychologist, on being presented with the same set of symptoms (for the same person) on a different occasion, would give the same diagnosis again

Cultural factors affecting the diagnosis of mental health issues

Cultural factors create problems with diagnosis and are a source of bias. Cultural and sub-cultural differences (i.e. within a culture), rather than an illness, may be the cause of problems, but these differences may not be recognised within that culture and a problem may be diagnosed as one of mental health.

A classification system used in one culture might not be appropriate in another. Davison and Neale (1994) give an example, and explain how not expressing emotions might be normal in one culture but seen as a symptom of mental illness in another. Sabin (1975) reminds us that language difficulties and differences might mean misleading translation of symptoms, which could lead to misdiagnosis. Patients from one culture may not confide in clinicians from another culture.

Many of these factors mean that mental illnesses are likely to be over-diagnosed for certain sections of the population. One example, given by Malgady et al. (1987), is the belief held by some Puerto Ricans that people can become possessed by evil spirits. If people from that culture talk about being possessed, it does not mean they are schizophrenic, but they might be diagnosed as such if their culture is not taken into account. Note that not all Hispanic peoples have this 'evil spirits' belief, so stereo-typing can easily occur, also leading to misdiagnosis.

In China, illness is seen as involving the balance (or imbalance) between Yin and Yang. Treatments reflect this belief, as would a Chinese classification system. This underlines the importance of taking beliefs and customs into account when diagnosing mental illness.

Evaluation

– Lopez (1989) offers a note of caution in suggesting that if we are too careful to take culture and beliefs into account, we may under-diagnose a particular illness.
– If people are not diagnosed as being schizophrenic, for example, because it is thought that they are hearing voices as part of their belief system, then they may miss out on necessary treatment (if they actually have schizophrenia).
– It is thought that there is more likely to be over-diagnosis in this country than under-diagnosis. For example, more West Indians in Britain are diagnosed as having mental illness than any other group, and this is likely to be due to misunderstanding of cultural issues.
– Blake (1973) found that in the USA, African-Americans are more likely to be diagnosed as schizophrenic than white Americans, which reflects the British findings, and again suggests cultural bias in diagnosis.

Summary

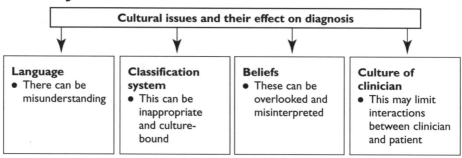

Cultural issues and their effect on diagnosis			
Language • There can be misunderstanding	**Classification system** • This can be inappropriate and culture-bound	**Beliefs** • These can be overlooked and misinterpreted	**Culture of clinician** • This may limit interactions between clinician and patient

Approaches and therapies

For this part of the clinical psychology application, you need to recall information about the main approaches to mental illness and mental health that you studied at AS: the physiological (medical/biological) approach, the psychodynamic approach, the learning (behaviourist) approach and the cognitive approach. The humanistic approach and, to an extent, the focus on the social approach are new.

You also need to compare different approaches to mental disorders. At the end of this Content Guidance section, there is a table comparing all the approaches in the specification.

Tip

Spend a few moments recalling the main assumptions of each approach before you read about how each of the four approaches you have already studied explains mental illness.

The medical/biological approach

The medical/biological approach to mental health issues assumes that there is a disease to be treated. Etiology is the study of what causes the disease, including genetic and biochemical factors. Medical terminology, such as illness, cure, pathological, symptoms, diagnosis, therapies, treatments and hospitals, is commonly used in connection with mental health issues and abnormal behaviour, as emphasised by Maher (1966).

Causes of mental health problems

The medical/biological approach focuses on disruptions of biological functioning (problems with neurotransmitters and messages, for example) and there is an assumption that this can be sorted out by biological means. The role of genes is an important part of this approach, and both the genotype (our genetic make up) and the phenotype (what we become as our genotype interacts with environmental factors) are studied. Many disorders involve the phenotype, as environmental influences are strong and can trigger or be the cause of a mental health problem. Other disorders stem directly from the genotype. Twin, family and adoption studies can help shed light on such issues. Disorders can also be caused by biochemical imbalance or by structural differences/problems in the brain.

> **Tip**
> Recall what you learnt about twin, family and adoption studies, including the problems of such methods. This will help you to evaluate the medical/biological model.

Examples of mental disorders with medical/biological causes

The following are examples of medical/biological causes attributed to mental health problems:

- Schizophrenia is said to have, at least in part, a genetic cause.
- Some faulty thinking processes are thought to be caused by brain damage.
- Depression can be said to be caused, again at least in part, by faulty neuronal transmission.
- Anxiety disorders could stem from problems in the autonomic nervous system, for example when a person is too easily aroused.

> **Tip**
> The sections on two specific mental disorders (pp. 48–50 and 55–57) consider evidence concerning possible genetic and other medical/biological causes. That evidence can be used both to explain and to evaluate the medical/biological approach to mental illness. For example, there are genetic, neurochemical and neurological explanations for schizophrenia.

Summary

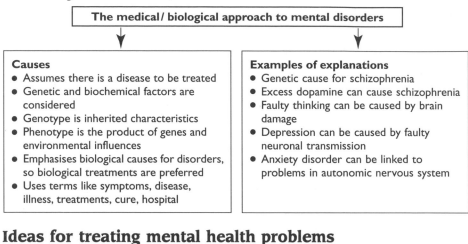

The medical / biological approach to mental disorders

Causes
- Assumes there is a disease to be treated
- Genetic and biochemical factors are considered
- Genotype is inherited characteristics
- Phenotype is the product of genes and environmental influences
- Emphasises biological causes for disorders, so biological treatments are preferred
- Uses terms like symptoms, disease, illness, treatments, cure, hospital

Examples of explanations
- Genetic cause for schizophrenia
- Excess dopamine can cause schizophrenia
- Faulty thinking can be caused by brain damage
- Depression can be caused by faulty neuronal transmission
- Anxiety disorder can be linked to problems in autonomic nervous system

Ideas for treating mental health problems

Treatments can include altering bodily functioning, perhaps using drugs to correct a perceived neurotransmitter imbalance. One example is when diazepam (Valium) is used to reduce tension in anxiety disorders. There can also be physical intervention, like surgery or electroconvulsive therapy (ECT).

Evaluation

+ Being diagnosed with a recognisable illness can sometimes be useful in terms of getting treatment and/or help.

+ It seems that individuals often feel more comfortable when a problem is labelled, partly because they then hope for suitable treatment (and a cure) and partly because they can then discuss their problems with others in terms that are understood.

− There are many diseases and symptoms, and symptoms overlap, so it is hard to be precise about a cause. Symptoms are externally visible features, but one symptom might not have a single cause. This tends to make conclusions simplistic, as the complexity is hard to grasp.

− Labelling someone as having a medical illness can be detrimental to how that person functions.

− Research data tend to be quantitative, although with mental health problems qualitative data might be more useful, given the complexity of the individual, and of the phenotype.

− The medical model assumes that objective measurements are used, such as scans and tests, whereas information for diagnosis often comes from interviews and observation. So the diagnosis and treatment might not be as clear-cut as the medical model suggests, and problems with reliability and validity (and cultural issues) might occur.

− If a disease is only known by its symptoms (e.g. schizophrenia) and is defined by them too, symptoms cannot prove the disease or vice versa. Diagnosis simply becomes a grouping of symptoms, and this does not prove a cause, although it might be useful in the approach to treatment(s). For example, someone having hallucinations and content guidance

being withdrawn is diagnosed as being schizophrenic, and it is said that he has the hallucinations and is withdrawn because of the schizophrenia, but this does not help at all with the cause (or treatment).
- There is a feeling that one 'illness' or label must have one cause, but in fact that may not be the case.
- Szasz (1960) argues against calling mental health problems 'diseases' because diseases refer to physical and not mental problems. Such problems concern how someone lives and a medical/biological approach will not help, according to this argument.

Therapies

| Tip |

Therapies for two disorders (schizophrenia and mood disorders) are presented here. These are the two specific mental disorders that are covered later in this guide, and so using them here will reduce the amount of material you need to cover.

Biological treatments: the use of drugs

Schizophrenia

Tranquillisers (phenothiazines) were first used in the treatment of schizophrenia. Chlorpromazine is an anti-psychotic drug, which reduces hallucinations and delusions, and is used in the treatment of schizophrenia.

Unipolar disorders

Unipolar disorders (e.g. depression) are often treated by drugs such as tricyclic anti-depressants, monoamine oxidase inhibitors (MAOs) and selective serotonin reuptake inhibitors (SSRIs) such as Prozac. These drugs often work at the synapse where neuro-transmitters are passing across from the axon of one neurone to the receptors of another neurone. Some drugs prevent reuptake: they leave the neurotransmitter to pass its signal via the receptors of the receiving neurone but inhibit the reuptake pumps which would remove it from the synaptic gap. Some drugs excite neuronal activity; some inhibit activity.

Bipolar disorders

Bipolar disorders (e.g. manic depression) are generally treated by lithium carbonate, which has the effect of flattening emotional responses. Episodes recur if it is stopped — as is the case with many of the drug treatments given for unipolar disorders.

| Evaluation |

+ Drug treatments do work for some disorders, e.g. bipolar disorders.
+ Drug treatments can work quite quickly, which gives a respite while a different or complementary treatment is considered. For example, depression can be treated with antidepressants for short-term relief, which can enable people to get to grips with other treatments, such as counselling, because they feel calmer.
+ Some might say that drug treatment is quick and easy for medical professionals.
+ Drugs do seem to be effective; for example, they reduce the anxiety felt during panic attacks (Ballenger et al. 1988).

± Drugs can be prescribed quite quickly and long consultations that might be needed for some forms of counselling or cognitive behavioural therapy are avoided. To this extent the treatment can be seen as cheap, although drugs themselves can be costly.

– It is possible that the use of drugs masks the problem but does not treat it. One symptom can simply replace another. Kane et al. (1988) found that between 10% and 20% of people do not improve if given drug therapy (although this presumably means that the others do improve in some way).

– Drugs may treat the symptoms, but it is doubtful if they address the cause of the disorder. Often the patient has to continue using the drugs, despite problems of dependency, tolerance and toxicity.

– Withdrawal symptoms can occur if drugs are discontinued, and there is often a relapse too. Hogarty (1984) claimed that 40% of patients relapsed within 6 months and 70% within 1 year. This means that drug treatment has to continue, which can be difficult if there is, for example, tolerance. Tolerance means that more and more of the drug is needed to achieve the same effect. Addiction can also occur.

– Side effects can be a problem. Drugs often act by mimicking or blocking neurotransmitter movements in some way. A neurotransmitter is likely to have many roles in the nervous system. The drug might help with some of the symptoms of the illness, but may also affect other functions of the nervous system. Anti-psychotic drugs, for example, can lead to tremors and jerking.

– Lithium carbonate can lead to dependency and, once started, the treatment must be continued. In addition, it does not work for everyone and can prove toxic.

Summary

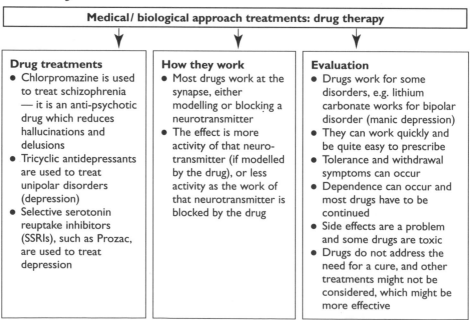

Medical/ biological approach treatments: drug therapy		
Drug treatments	**How they work**	**Evaluation**
• Chlorpromazine is used to treat schizophrenia — it is an anti-psychotic drug which reduces hallucinations and delusions • Tricyclic antidepressants are used to treat unipolar disorders (depression) • Selective serotonin reuptake inhibitors (SSRIs), such as Prozac, are used to treat depression	• Most drugs work at the synapse, either modelling or blocking a neurotransmitter • The effect is more activity of that neurotransmitter (if modelled by the drug), or less activity as the work of that neurotransmitter is blocked by the drug	• Drugs work for some disorders, e.g. lithium carbonate works for bipolar disorder (manic depression) • They can work quickly and be quite easy to prescribe • Tolerance and withdrawal symptoms can occur • Dependence can occur and most drugs have to be continued • Side effects are a problem and some drugs are toxic • Drugs do not address the need for a cure, and other treatments might not be considered, which might be more effective

The psychodynamic approach

Tip

Recall what you learnt about psychoanalytic theory for AS, including what Freud suggested and the criticisms of his views. This will help you to understand and evaluate the psychodynamic approach to mental disorders.

Causes of mental health problems

According to the psychodynamic approach, problems come from unconscious forces within the individual. These are not (by definition) known to the individual, as they are kept hidden by means of such devices as defence mechanisms. Using (unconsciously) defence mechanisms to protect our conscious selves from threatening thoughts uses energy. This use of energy can mean that we are not functioning well in our lives — that we have a mental disorder. We are busy repressing unwanted thoughts and desires, instead of moving on.

Thoughts are pushed into the unconscious because they are threatening. This idea of what is threatening can come from parents and society — rules that we have to follow. From birth to approximately 1 year old, we are ruled by our id (our instinctive desires), which works on a pleasure principle. As we learn that we cannot always have what we want immediately, we develop our ego (from around 2 years old), which works on a reality principle — for example, we have to wait to satisfy our desires, and we learn to wait. From about the age of 4 or 5 years our parents have instilled in us social rules, and we develop a superego, which is a conscience and an idea of what we should be like.

According to this view, our personality comprises the demanding id, the reasoning ego and the controlling superego. The aim is to have a 'balanced' personality, meaning that the ego can balance the possibly irrational demands of the id against the controlling demands of the superego.

The paragraphs above focus on the traditional psychodynamic approach, and Freud's views. Others have built on these views, but built in differences. Jung, for example, emphasised decision-making and goal-setting, and the importance of looking forward as well as back. He thought that to understand people it was important to understand their dreams and aspirations as well as their past history.

Erikson also built on psychodynamic principles but focused more on social aspects of development, extending the idea of development in stages. He proposed eight psychosocial stages — the 'Eight Stages of Man' — covering the whole life span — from birth to death. In each stage there are conflicts to overcome; for example, the first stage leads to the learning of trust or mistrust, and the last stage involves achieving integrity or despair. Mental health is achieved by negotiating these stages successfully.

Summary

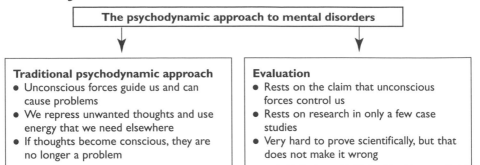

The psychodynamic approach to mental disorders

Traditional psychodynamic approach
- Unconscious forces guide us and can cause problems
- We repress unwanted thoughts and use energy that we need elsewhere
- If thoughts become conscious, they are no longer a problem

Evaluation
- Rests on the claim that unconscious forces control us
- Rests on research in only a few case studies
- Very hard to prove scientifically, but that does not make it wrong

Therapies

Psychoanalysis

The obvious therapy to consider within this approach is psychoanalysis; you will already know quite a lot about this from your AS studies. It will also be useful because it could be considered as a way of treating mood disorders or schizophrenia (the two mental disorders that are studied later in this guide). However, you should note that the psychodynamic approach is not generally used to explain either mood disorders or schizophrenia, not at least by most clinical psychologists and psychiatrists.

Aim

The aim of psychoanalysis is to release unconscious thoughts and make them conscious. The individual can then recognise these thoughts, which will no longer be repressed and causing a problem — at least that is the theory. Hypnosis, therefore, is not useful, as the patients will not be consciously aware of what they are saying, so will possibly not admit that what was said is true when it is relayed by the psycho-analyst — in other words, they might continue to repress those thoughts.

Method

Psychoanalysis involves a 'talking cure'. The psychoanalyst allots a set amount of time (say an hour) to listening to the client. Unlike some psychotherapies, where the therapist might be more active, the analyst listens and interprets, but the important data come from the flow of thoughts from the analysand (person being analysed). Transference, where the analysand transfers feelings onto the analyst, is a key part of the process. These can be feelings of love or hate, and they help in releasing unconscious thoughts.

Methods used within psychoanalysis within a single case study involve dream analysis, if appropriate, or free association. Dream analysis involves analysing dreams to look for themes or hidden meanings. The manifest content of the dream is what the person is telling the analyst about. The latent content is what is hidden within the dream, by means of symbols, for example. This involves skilled analysis and an understanding of the person's background etc. Free association involves the client saying whatever comes to mind.

Both dream analysis and free association (and analysis of any slips of the tongue that might occur, such as calling someone by the wrong name) are ways of accessing the unconscious, which is otherwise unreachable.

Themes and symbols are analysed to try to put together a picture of what is being repressed. It is important that the clients 'buy into' the analysis, as they must accept the picture, to make the unconscious thoughts conscious.

Uses of psychoanalysis

Psychotherapy is used in the treatment of mood disorders and schizophrenia, but based on the humanistic approach (outlined on pp. 36–38) and not on psychodynamic theory. This is mainly because it is not popularly thought that there is a psychodynamic explanation for mood disorders or schizophrenia. Psychoanalysis is used to treat problems with functioning, including anxiety and phobias.

The psychoanalytic approach is sometimes used to explain schizophrenia, suggesting that the delusions and thought disorders characteristic of schizophrenia might be evidence of repression or regression. Regression involves going back to a state of being under the influence of the id's demands, and not having the superego's controlling influence. Repression refers to keeping unwanted thoughts in the unconscious.

Object relations psychotherapy

Psychodynamic theorists have moved on from Freud and there are now other psycho-analytic therapies, such as object relations. Object relations psychotherapy is a type of psychoanalytic theory that looks at representations of the self and others. The objects themselves (self and others) are not as interesting as the fantasies and emotions that go with them — which affect how people relate to others. Deprivation and abuse in childhood are seen as important, as is attachment theory. Heinz Kohut and Otto Kernberg are theorists in this area. For example, Kernberg (1985) claims that borderline personality disorder comes with weak egos. People with this disorder are not comfortable when being asked about childhood conflicts, as happens in psycho-analysis.

Therapy focuses on the way those with borderline personality disorder tend to charac-terise things as good or bad, rather than seeing all the degrees of positive and negative in between (this is called 'splitting'). If people see the world and others in black and white terms, they have problems in relating to others (problems with object relations). It is thought that they maintain a simple outlook on life (e.g. good/bad) in order to protect their ego and make decisions easier. They need to be helped to see things in a more complex way. Kernberg is willing to direct his patients towards this goal, and in this way is different from traditional psychoanalysts, who try to be less directive.

Evaluation

+ Those who are able to be rational and use words well can benefit from psycho-analysis. This means that neuroses rather than psychoses are treated in this way. Psychoses generally involve the person being unaware, at least in part, of their illness, whereas those with neuroses tend to know about it. The 'talking cure' tends to work best for someone who can verbalise problems well, such as describing dreams that are considered relevant.

+ The approach does not involve taking medication, and does not lead to consequent side effects (though there can be effects for the client, as demonstrated by false memory syndrome).

+ In some ways, it could be said that the clients cure themselves, and so it is likely that any solution will be lasting.

+ The psychodynamic approach may be useful simply in shifting the focus from biological explanations to look at emotions as possible causes of mental disorders.

− Psychoanalysis is not likely to be useful for children, as it involves some self-analysis. (However, the idea of analysing behaviour to look for underlying symbols and themes is found in play therapy.)

− Psychoanalysis is quite time-consuming — the client often needs numerous sessions with the analyst before anything is achieved. This makes it expensive too.

− It seems to be limited to those who can afford it, who have the time, who can verbalise well and who have some understanding of their problem.

− It rests on the idea that unconscious wishes, thoughts and desires are holding us back and can be a cause of mental disorders such as phobias and neuroses, for example obsessive-compulsive disorder. If this idea is criticised, then the treatment can be criticised too. This means that any criticisms of the approach itself (e.g. it rests on limited case studies in a specific culture) can be used to criticise this treatment. Freud took few notes when he carried out his case studies, so he relied on memory, which we could claim must affect the reliability of the case studies. In addition, he may well have affected what his patients were saying. For example, because Freud was so interested in childhood events, his patients are likely to have focused on these. Freud also used only a small number of case studies yet generalised his findings to say that they apply to the whole population. This generalisation can be criticised as not justified.

− The analyst has to infer a great deal from what the client is saying. Such inference is subjective and may be biased, which some might say detracts from the findings.

Summary

Psychodynamic approach treatments: psychoanalysis

Traditional psychoanalysis	Evaluation
• The analyst takes a back seat and lets the client talk to try to unearth unconscious thoughts • This is done by means of a clinical interview/case study, and within that dream analysis, free association, slips of the tongue etc. might help to reveal repressed thoughts within the unconscious • Once the unconscious thoughts have been revealed, the person has them in the conscious and there should no longer be problems	• Problems with this approach affect the usefulness of the treatment • Psychoanalysis can lead to false memories and can be damaging • It takes a long time and can be expensive • It is limited to certain people and certain problems

The behavioural approach

Tip
You will need to refer back to the learning approach that you studied at AS. Both classical and operant conditioning can be called 'behavioural'. Social learning theory also draws on behaviourist principles, while including other mechanisms as well. Recall the mechanisms of these forms of learning now.

According to this approach, mental disorders are characterised by maladaptive (unsuitable) behaviour. Abnormality is when someone shows maladaptive behaviour that somehow interferes with normal functioning. It is not that much different from normality — just somewhere further along a line between what is normal and what is abnormal.

This approach focuses on problematic behaviour, rather than on the emotions and thoughts of the individual concerned. If it is the behaviour that is the problem, for example, someone with obsessive-compulsive disorder (OCD) shows maladaptive behaviour, then changing the behaviour (stopping it from being a problem) can solve the disorder.

Causes of mental health problems

The reason for the maladaptive behaviour is that it has been learnt wrongly. That learning must be changed — and replaced with new, suitable learning. Behaviourist theories suggest ways that learning can be changed. This can be by behaviour modification, which links to classical conditioning mechanisms, or by behaviour therapy, which links to operant conditioning mechanisms.

Classical conditioning works with involuntary (reflex) behaviour, and new associations must be learnt, for example for phobias.

Operant conditioning works with voluntary behaviours. Shaping new behaviour by means of positive and negative reinforcement is a way of replacing the old, unwanted behaviour with new, desirable patterns.

Examples of mental disorders linked to maladaptive behaviours

Phobias

Phobias are thought to be classically conditioned, whereby a natural fear response that occurs to a natural phenomenon then starts to occur in response to something else, having been associated with it in some way. For example, a natural fear response to someone shouting starts occurring whenever someone goes into a certain building, because that building (e.g. a school) is associated with the shouting.

Watson and Rayner's (1920) study of Little Albert showed how classical conditioning could lead to a phobia. They deliberately banged a metal bar behind a baby's head to make a very loud noise and startle him. They did this when he was playing with a pet rat, but not, for example, when he was playing with building blocks. Because of the noise, he showed a startle response when playing with the rat, and not when playing with the blocks. Soon there was no need for the noise — Little Albert showed a startle response just when the rat was present — he had learnt to associate fear with the rat.

Depression

Depression could occur as a result of operant conditioning principles. Some people might go out less, and do less than others, so would possibly get less positive reinforcement. Lewinsohn (1974) suggests that as reinforcement is reduced the individual will respond less to others, and finally depression will occur. This explanation is explored in more detail on pp. 59–60.

Evaluation

+ Behaviour is observable, even though this must be done carefully. So maladaptive behaviour(s) can be observed and logged, and then steps taken to change it. The new behaviour(s) can also be observed and logged. The clients themselves can see changes.
+ Treatments stemming from the behavioural approach have been found to be effective. For example, aversion therapy and token economy programmes have been said to be useful. Therapies are considered on pp. 31–32.
− If depression were to be considered as being caused by maladaptive learning (as outlined above), then this would take a long time to record and measure. There are many factors to consider and lots of different patterns of reinforcement.
− It would be hard to show that maladaptive learning was the only cause of a mental disorder.
− Monozygotic (MZ) twins are identical (share 100% of their genetic make-up). If MZ twins were both schizophrenic, a learning theorist could say that this showed that the problem stemmed from their pattern of reinforcements which would be similar. However, if MZ twins were not both schizophrenic, but only one was, the learning theorist could claim that one had experienced a different pattern of reinforcements. Looking at patterns of reinforcements is too general and could be used to explain every situation — so it may be seen as not very useful.
− If therapy based on learning theory is effective (e.g. giving positive reinforcement for certain behaviours, as in a token economy programme) this does not mean that the cause of the problem can be explained using behaviourist principles — they might help with the solution, without being anything to do with the cause.
− One strength of this approach is that it focuses on observable and measurable behaviours. However, the weakness is that it does not look at emotional or cognitive processes — or indeed at biological ones. This seems rather limiting, as some mental disorders have a biological cause, an emotional cause or are the result of faulty thinking.

Summary

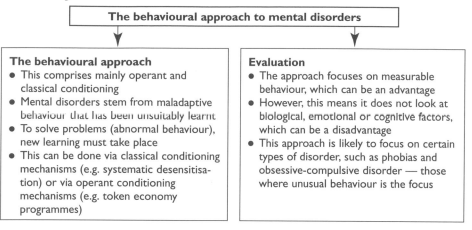

The behavioural approach to mental disorders

The behavioural approach
- This comprises mainly operant and classical conditioning
- Mental disorders stem from maladaptive behaviour that has been unsuitably learnt
- To solve problems (abnormal behaviour), new learning must take place
- This can be done via classical conditioning mechanisms (e.g. systematic desensitisation) or via operant conditioning mechanisms (e.g. token economy programmes)

Evaluation
- The approach focuses on measurable behaviour, which can be an advantage
- However, this means it does not look at biological, emotional or cognitive factors, which can be a disadvantage
- This approach is likely to focus on certain types of disorder, such as phobias and obsessive-compulsive disorder — those where unusual behaviour is the focus

Therapies

Tip

You will have studied ways of modifying human behaviour when doing the AS part of the course, so it would be useful to revise those therapies here, rather than to learn new ones. Systematic desensitisation to help with phobias and token economy programmes to help with maladaptive behaviour are often covered at AS, so those two therapies are described here. Note that you only need one of these for the exam, but knowing both will help in outlining and criticising this approach to mental disorders.

Behaviour modification: systematic desensitisation

Systematic desensitisation is based on classical conditioning principles. Counter-conditioning suggests that one response to a stimulus can be replaced by another response — for example, a fear response can be replaced by a relaxation response. Systematic desensitisation works on this counterconditioning principle.

First, the person needs to be able to relax deeply, and that is practised. Then the therapist and client think about the feared object or situation and make a list working from the least feared (perhaps a picture) to the most feared (such as touching the live object). Finally, the client works through each step of the list in his/her imagination, keeping as relaxed as possible at the same time. The client learns to stay relaxed and to replace the fear response with the more relaxed response. The behaviour (in this case a fear response) will no longer be maladaptive.

Evaluation

+ This technique has been shown to work.
+ It rests on quite sound theory that can be explained to the client. This might help with its success, as it is understandable, so the client can work with the therapist to achieve a cure, and can practise outside the sessions.

– Even if the technique works, it does not mean that a cure has taken place. Some might argue that if the cause is not addressed, any improvement in quality of living might not last and does not represent a cure.

    – It can be time-consuming and expensive, as around ten sessions might be necessary.

Behaviour therapy: token economy programmes (TEPs)

Token economy programmes are based on operant conditioning principles. The idea was developed in mental institutions to encourage more appropriate behaviour in those with severe mental disorders. There are rules about what rewards are to be given for which behaviours. As the name suggests, rewards are tokens that can be exchanged for 'real' goods or privileges.

Evaluation

+ The therapy is fairly cheap to carry out compared, perhaps, with drug treatments.

+ Results are visible and measurable.

– It may be hard for the patient to continue with the desired (shaped) behaviour outside the institution, as the system is so closely linked to the institution and its staff, and rewards would not continue outside.

– Members of staff need training and it might be hard for all staff to follow the same rules precisely, which could be confusing for patients.

– There is a problem with social control. The staff have control and shape the patient's behaviour, which might not be seen as an ethical thing to do. There is also the problem of who decides what is appropriate behaviour and what is not. Some may regard members of staff as abusing their power.

Summary

Behavioural approach treatments: two therapies

Classical conditioning: systematic desensitisation

- Patients are taught to relax deeply and then draw up a list of different forms of the feared objects, from the least feared to the most feared
- Then they imagine each part of the list from the least to the most feared while maintaining a relaxed state
- They replace the maladaptive fear response with an appropriate relaxed response

Evaluation

- This takes time and may need around ten sessions
- It relies on patients being able to imagine, and being able to help themselves
- It really only works for certain problems, such as phobias

Operant conditioning: TEPs

- Instigated in mental institutions to improve behaviour
- Tokens given as positive reinforcement for appropriate behaviour are exchanged for items or privileges

Evaluation

- The desired behaviour may not be transferred when the person leaves the mental institution
- Staff have a lot of power, which may be misused; who decides what behaviour is appropriate?

The cognitive approach

> **Tip**
>
> You studied the cognitive approach for AS, so it is a good idea to recall the basic assumptions now.

The cognitive approach looks at thought processes. According to this approach, we do not learn passively as the behavioural approach suggests. On the contrary, we are active when learning — we are thinking and using cognitive processes such as attention and memory.

The cognitive approach suggests that thought processes are involved, and that they are somehow causing mental disorders. An example would be attending to particular thoughts (e.g. destructive ones) rather than to others (e.g. more positive ones). Remembering negative events can be a cause of mental disorders, and more positive events may be overlooked. Our perceptions are affected by previous experiences as well, so there may be a cognitive explanation for why a mental disorder continues.

Depression is an example of a disorder that can be explained by reference to principles within the cognitive approach. If depression involves negative thought patterns, which it seems to, then encouraging positive thinking might be one way of helping someone to overcome depression.

Cognitive restructuring can be a good way of overcoming disorders such as depression. In cognitive-behavioural therapy, changing thought processes is believed to change behaviour and emotions.

> **Evaluation**
>
> + There is common-sense appeal in suggesting that mental disorders not only involve faulty thinking or negative thinking patterns, but also could be caused by these negative patterns. 'Positive thinking' has become a well-known phrase that seems to be accepted as helping with 'normal' thinking patterns.
> ± Therapies such as cognitive-behavioural therapies tend to emphasise both changing thought patterns and changing behaviour, so the cognitive and behavioural approaches are not kept completely separate. This is not really a weakness, but needs to be remembered — often cognitive processes are just considered on their own.
> − Cognitive restructuring suggests that individuals need to be able to access their thought processes, and be able to change them, which might not be possible in some disorders, such as psychoses like schizophrenia. There are those, however, who think that cognitive therapy can help with schizophrenia, which after all is characterised by faulty thinking.

Summary

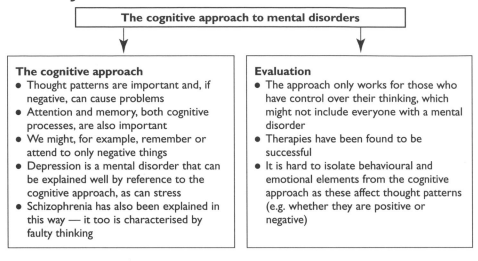

The cognitive approach to mental disorders

The cognitive approach
- Thought patterns are important and, if negative, can cause problems
- Attention and memory, both cognitive processes, are also important
- We might, for example, remember or attend to only negative things
- Depression is a mental disorder that can be explained well by reference to the cognitive approach, as can stress
- Schizophrenia has also been explained in this way — it too is characterised by faulty thinking

Evaluation
- The approach only works for those who have control over their thinking, which might not include everyone with a mental disorder
- Therapies have been found to be successful
- It is hard to isolate behavioural and emotional elements from the cognitive approach as these affect thought patterns (e.g. whether they are positive or negative)

Therapies

Tip

Depression is focused upon here (with some comments about schizophrenia). It is one of the two mental disorders studied on pp. 54–61.

Rational-emotive behaviour therapy

Ellis (1962) suggests that irrational beliefs cause maladaptive behaviour. If people have mistaken beliefs about what they should be achieving, they can put pressure on themselves and give themselves unreasonable goals to achieve.

Rational-emotive therapy requires that people look at what they expect of themselves, and think more rationally. For example, they must admit that they can make mistakes — something that some people find hard to accept. People are also helped to adjust emotionally. As the therapy focuses on reasoning processes and emotional responses, as well as behaviour, it is called rational-emotive behaviour therapy. For example, if people say to a therapist that nothing goes right for them, the therapist can work with them to move away from this generalisation by identifying something that *has* gone right.

Cognitive-behaviour therapy

Beck (1967) emphasises how problems can develop when people distort their experiences. Someone who is depressed is likely to see only the bad things that happen. Cognitive therapy asks people to think again about their experiences and focus less on bad ones — or see them as less bad.

Beck used a behavioural approach too in suggesting that a way of preventing negative thinking is to do something active, such as going for a walk. By doing active things there is the possibility of positive reinforcement when things go well (e.g. if people enjoy the walk or parts of it) and this helps with positive thinking.

Evaluation

+ The individual is helped to recognise any problems and is taught to overcome difficulties, so it is likely that any solutions will be more lasting than a therapy such as token economy which is outside the individual's own control.

+ Cognitive restructuring has been successfully used, for example, in stress management. By having a sense of control, a person is better able to cope with stressful situations.

+ Rush et al. (1977) found that cognitive therapy was more successful in alleviating bipolar depression than using tricyclic imipramine (drug therapy). Other studies have also found that cognitive therapy works for depression (e.g. Seligman et al., 1988).

– The therapies rely on rational individuals who can control their thought patterns, at least to an extent, so may only be suitable for certain individuals. Young children or people with psychoses may not respond to cognitive therapies.

– Evaluations have supported the usefulness of cognitive therapies for depression, but there are other studies that suggest that either a mix of therapies (e.g. cognitive therapy and drug therapy) would be more successful or that other therapies such as social skills training might be more useful. Haaga and Davison (1989) found that it was important that the treatment matched the individual — someone with irrational thinking benefits from cognitive therapy, but someone with a social skills deficit benefits from social skills training.

Summary

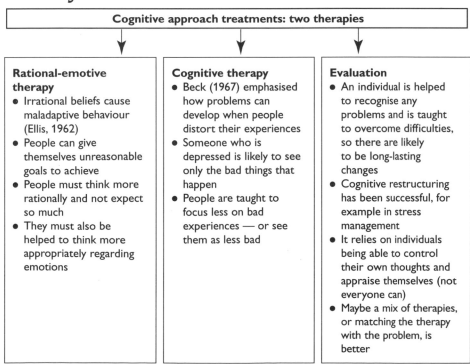

Cognitive approach treatments: two therapies		
Rational-emotive therapy • Irrational beliefs cause maladaptive behaviour (Ellis, 1962) • People can give themselves unreasonable goals to achieve • People must think more rationally and not expect so much • They must also be helped to think more appropriately regarding emotions	**Cognitive therapy** • Beck (1967) emphasised how problems can develop when people distort their experiences • Someone who is depressed is likely to see only the bad things that happen • People are taught to focus less on bad experiences — or see them as less bad	**Evaluation** • An individual is helped to recognise any problems and is taught to overcome difficulties, so there are likely to be long-lasting changes • Cognitive restructuring has been successful, for example in stress management • It relies on individuals being able to control their own thoughts and appraise themselves (not everyone can) • Maybe a mix of therapies, or matching the therapy with the problem, is better

content guidance

The humanistic approach

The focus of the humanistic approach is on personal growth and reaching our potential. It sees human nature as basically good and assumes that we all have the goal to self-actualise (or reach our own potential). According to this approach, mental disorder is due to this growth or potential being disrupted for some reason. The approach emphasises:

- free will — we are seen as free to fulfil our potential. (This is different from the deterministic approach of the biological, behaviourist and psychodynamic approaches.)
- our strengths, not our weaknesses. (Our own view of our world is what matters, not anyone else's view.)

It focuses on mental health and what is needed to achieve it, rather than disorders. Therapies are sometimes called existential therapies. Carl Rogers and Abraham Maslow are two key names in the humanistic approach.

Evaluation

- + The positive attitude within this approach is encouraging, holding, as it does, that everyone has the goal to self-actualise and the ability within themselves to do so. This positive attitude is carried over into therapies and in itself can do good.
- + Nicolson and Berman (1983) found that the positive effects of therapy lasted many months after the treatment had stopped.
- ± Simply undergoing therapy might be helpful and might have a placebo effect.
- − The approach assumes that people are inherently good, although there is little evidence for this.
- − It might be more useful for neuroses and certain mental disorders where individuals are able to appraise their feelings and work to change than for psychoses where individuals are not so aware of their problems.
- − Having a sympathetic listener might act as positive reinforcement, and so the success of the therapy can be explained in behaviourist terms, not humanistic ones.

— The approach does not explain how faulty reasoning takes place, if we are all naturally motivated to self-actualise.

Summary

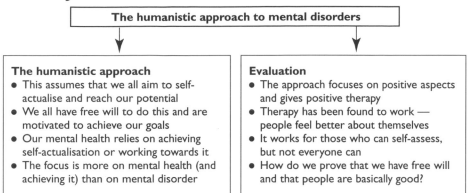

The humanistic approach	Evaluation
• This assumes that we all aim to self-actualise and reach our potential • We all have free will to do this and are motivated to achieve our goals • Our mental health relies on achieving self-actualisation or working towards it • The focus is more on mental health (and achieving it) than on mental disorder	• The approach focuses on positive aspects and gives positive therapy • Therapy has been found to work — people feel better about themselves • It works for those who can self-assess, but not everyone can • How do we prove that we have free will and that people are basically good?

Therapies

Client-centred therapy

This therapy was proposed by Carl Rogers. Therapists need to create a situation where clients can become mentally healthy, but the individuals must do this for themselves. Giving individuals unconditional positive regard enables them to explore their feelings and goals in a safe place with support. If they can avoid demands from others, they can tap into their innate drive to self-actualise. The therapist creates a situation where individuals can be themselves, away from constraints.

Three core qualities for the therapist are genuineness (the therapist must be normal and honest), unconditional positive regard (there must be no conditions — the client will be liked whatever the circumstances) and accurate empathic understanding (the therapist must see the world through the eyes of the client).

> **Evaluation**

+ Clients gain self-knowledge and so the therapy effects are more likely to be transferred into their own environment away from the therapy sessions. This is not the case for all therapies (e.g. token economy programmes).
− It is not easy for the therapist to give unconditional positive regard as the therapist may not like the client, or may be horrified by what the client says or has done. In these cases (as therapists must be honest too), it may be necessary for the therapist to transfer the client to someone else, and this rejection could be harmful.
− Evaluation tends to rely on self-reports, which in turn focus on how the clients feel. Their actual behaviour after therapy is not usually studied, so it is hard to see how far the clients actually change as a result of therapy. Evaluating how a person feels is not easy — how do we know data are valid? Individuals may say what they think they should say. Indeed, the clients might not know how they really feel themselves.

Summary

Humanistic approach treatments: one therapy

Client-centred therapy (Carl Rogers)	Evaluation
• A safe situation without social pressures is provided so that individuals can explore themselves and their goals • Therapists need unconditional positive regard, empathy and genuineness • Individuals can sort out their own preferences and needs	• The therapy has been shown to be successful even a few months after it has ceased • It focuses on positive elements, which is encouraging in itself • It might be only positive reinforcement that works, so more behavioural than humanistic • It is hard to give everyone unconditional positive regard

The social approach

Tip

You studied the social approach for AS Unit 1. Recall now that its main assumptions focus on the importance of interactions between people, and how they affect what we do and what we are like. It also emphasises the importance of groups — in other words, that we do not act as individuals without influences from society around us.

Those diagnosed with mental disorders live within a society, and that society affects how they are treated and how they behave. Treatments and therapies take place within social and cultural settings, and are affected by those settings.

The treatment of mental illness depends on the society or culture, as is shown when considering issues such as abnormality and diagnosis. It is important, therefore, to look at how social issues affect those diagnosed as mentally ill. Social issues concern interactions between people, but also include funding, health service decisions and ideas of what is important.

Community psychology examines the role of the environment, both in creating mental health problems and in providing solutions to them. It also looks at preventing problems and links to health psychology, for example focusing on health and prevention of problems and health education programmes. Social trends such as 'care in the community' (discussed on p. 39–40) have led to a growth in community psychology.

Evaluation

+ The medical approach seems to ignore social factors that might be involved in the diagnosis of mental disorders. The social approach focuses on race, social class, environment and problems with living. This leads to more focus on prevention, which could be said to be better than 'cure'.
+ Drop-in centres and crisis prevention programmes appear to have had some success (see p. 40).

+ Day hospitals have allowed some family life to be maintained for certain patients, and for some that has been successful.
− The ideals behind care in the community programmes might be genuine, but social factors include political ones. There tends to be a problem when practical factors such as cost and number of health professionals available are confused with decisions taken for 'caring' reasons. Evaluation of programmes is often funded by government, and looks at issues such as cost and staffing, rather than focusing purely on how far a programme is successful in itself.
− There have been reported cases in which those who are mentally ill have failed to keep up with necessary medication and consequently have experienced problems. In these instances, it is said that community programmes have failed those in their care.

Summary

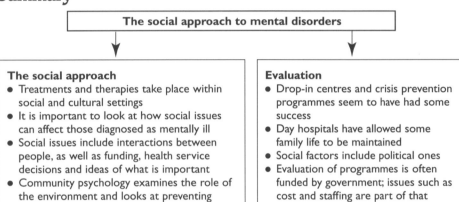

The social approach to mental disorders	
The social approach • Treatments and therapies take place within social and cultural settings • It is important to look at how social issues can affect those diagnosed as mentally ill • Social issues include interactions between people, as well as funding, health service decisions and ideas of what is important • Community psychology examines the role of the environment and looks at preventing problems and links to health psychology	**Evaluation** • Drop-in centres and crisis prevention programmes seem to have had some success • Day hospitals have allowed some family life to be maintained • Social factors include political ones • Evaluation of programmes is often funded by government; issues such as cost and staffing are part of that evaluation

Therapies

Care in the community

Care in the community programmes were developed in the early 1990s for various (often social) reasons:

• Mental hospitals were seen as expensive and ineffectual. If drugs could calm patients sufficiently, then perhaps they could manage in their own community.
• There was a shortage of trained therapists.
• As questions began to be asked about the role of social factors in causing mental health problems (such as pressures of living, or the need to adhere to certain social norms) the idea grew that solutions involving social factors should also be looked at.
• The medical approach was being questioned — social and environmental factors were seen as having a role in leading to mental health problems, so perhaps they should have a role in any solutions.

Care in the community programmes aimed to set up environments in which patients could be reintegrated into society and have a place in a community. For example, halfway houses help patients to move within society but still provide support. Day hospitals are also part of care in the community schemes. They enable someone to live at home while still having daily care — and they are less expensive than if someone is permanently in a hospital setting.

Drop-in centres/crisis prevention

Drop-in centres provide immediate access to care and are aimed at crisis prevention — stepping in to help before any problem or disorder becomes so bad that hospitalisation is needed. Centres in the community can be reached more easily, so, for example, people can get help when they are stressed — before this stress leads to a more serious mental illness. In some instances, telephone answering rather than walk-in services are provided.

Evaluation

+ Decker and Stubblebine (1972) found that there were fewer hospitalisations when crisis prevention was used.
+ Felner et al. (1991) suggest that prevention programmes are now more effective as learning has taken place from earlier models.
± 24-hour telephone services in drop-in centres can work if professionals take the calls, but are less effective with volunteers.
− To be effective, drop-in centres need to offer a 24-hour walk-in service, and give someone immediate attention. This is very hard to achieve in practice.
− If a continual drop-in service is possible, it is still difficult to get a broad medical opinion each time. Mental health professionals have to be very flexible in being able to deal with a wide variety of problems and situations, so there is a training issue.
− Rappaport (1977) found no evidence that community programmes improve people's mental health.

Summary

Social approach treatments: two therapies		
Care in the community • Mental hospitals were seen as expensive and ineffectual • If drugs could calm patients sufficiently, then perhaps they could manage in their own community • Halfway houses help patients to move within society but still with support • Day hospitals are also part of care in the community schemes	**Drop-in centres/crisis prevention** • Drop-in centres provide more immediate access to care and are aimed at crisis intervention • Centres in the community can be reached more easily, and problems can be stopped before they escalate • Sometimes telephone answering services are provided	**Evaluation** • 24-hour telephone services in drop-in centres can work if professionals take the calls, but are less effective with volunteers • Decker and Stubblebine (1972) found that there were fewer hospitalisations • Felner et al. (1991) suggested that prevention programmes are now more effective • Rappaport (1977) found no evidence that community programmes work

Comparing the six approaches

Problems with choosing a therapy or treatment

Clinical psychologists use a mixture of treatments and therapies.

- Even those diagnosed with the same disorder (e.g. depression) might have different symptoms (e.g. one person lacks the social skills to go out, whereas another has panic attacks) and they are likely, therefore, to need different therapeutic approaches.
- Different mental disorders have a different cause or causes and so require different therapeutic approaches.
- The same mental disorder (the diagnosis might just be a label) may have different causes, so different therapies would be needed for different patients.

The above points assume that:

- we know the cause for the disorder, which is by no means always the case. Clinicians might have to try treatments to see what effects they have, and to see if they can find something that works.
- the diagnosis is correct (reliable and valid). However, it has already been shown that this is by no means definite.

Some reasons for choosing one approach over another

Clinical psychologists' beliefs

Clinical psychologists have beliefs that stem from their own experiences and/or training which can affect their choice of treatment. Their beliefs about the cause of the problem are also likely to influence their choice of treatment. For example, phobias tend to lead on to systematic desensitisation or a learning theory treatment, whereas schizophrenia tends to be treated with anti-schizophrenic drugs. Custom and practice are also important.

Speed

Speed might be important. For example, it might be thought that psychotherapy would suit a particular individual, but not until the individual has calmed down a little, so drugs might be prescribed in the short term as they might be seen as faster acting.

Availability

Availability might be important. For example, the clinical psychologist might not know of an available psychoanalyst whom he or she feels would be suitable from a personality point of view.

Differences between the approaches

The above comments about problems with choosing treatments and reasons for choosing one treatment over another will have illustrated something about the differences between the approaches.

Table 2 summarises some basic differences — in assumptions, and treatments. Use the comments in the right-hand column to draw distinguishing points between the approaches.

Table 2 Comparing approaches to mental disorders

Approach	Assumptions about mental disorders	Treatments/ therapies	Comments
Medical/ biological	• Focuses on nervous system and genes; also on faulty neuronal transmission • Genotype (inherited charac-teristics) and phenotype (geno-type + environ-ment) are both important	• Drug therapy • Correcting/altering neurotransmitters • Corrective surgery • Biological/medical interventions	• Reductionist in focusing on underpinning biology • Biological cause leads to biological treatment • Accepts environmental factors and emotions as causes of mental disorders, but looks below them to a biological level for solution
Psychodynamic	• Unconscious thoughts guide behaviour • Repressed urges use up energy • By making uncon-scious thoughts conscious, we can move on	• Psychoanalysis involves a talking cure • The patient talks, especially about childhood • Patient and analyst examine what is said to reveal the problem through symbols	• Focuses on emotions rather than biology or behaviour • The theory is biological — about instincts, energy and urges • Accepts biological underpinning as a cause of problems, but focuses on emotional level for a solution
Behavioural	• Problems stem from maladaptive behaviour • New behaviour needs to be learnt • Based on classical and operant conditioning principles	• Systematic desen-sitisation is based on classical conditioning and can help with phobias • Token economy programmes are based on operant conditioning • Both involve replacing undesired with desired responses	• Ignores biological, emotional and most cognitive factors, but accepts an element of cognition • Applies well to some mental disorders, such as phobias and mal-adaptive (antisocial) behaviours • Does not apply to all mental disorders (although it is claimed that it does)

Approach	Assumptions about mental disorders	Treatments/ therapies	Comments
Cognitive	• Disorders are caused by faulty and negative thinking patterns, e.g. saying 'nothing goes right' can characterise depression	• Cognitive therapies involve people in analysing their thought processes and aiming for more positive thinking • Emotions can also be focused upon (to make them more positive) • Behaviour is not discounted, as it can encourage positive thoughts	• Cognitive therapies are wrapped up with behavioural ones — doing something to get positive reinforcement is seen by some (e.g. Beck) as advantageous • Emotions are accepted as important and positive thinking is a way of reducing stress and depression • Biological underpinning to mental disorders is not a consideration
Humanistic	• Mental health is the main aim • We all strive for self-actualisation • Mental health problems arise when reaching our goal(s) is frustrated in some way	• Client-centred therapy (on which counselling is based) aims to help someone self-actualise • Unconditional positive regard, empathy and genuineness help	• Focuses on the positive aspects of human nature, whereas the psychodynamic approach sees human nature as needing restraint • Biology is ignored except to say that we are inherently good • Emotions are important
Social	• Mental health problems have social bases too — race, class, environment, family • People live in a community, and so to be helped they need to be reintegrated into that community • Prevention is better than cure	• Community care programmes help with reintegration and quality of life, but may be a cheaper and less effective option • Drop-in facilities and crisis prevention try to stop problems from escalating by giving immediate support; this is hard to do and needs sufficient staff	• Social factors and practical skills are emphasised — along with emotional aspects • Biological basis is accepted but not focused upon; drug therapy is accepted • More a practical approach in helping people to deal with problems than a theoretical approach about the cause of mental illnesses

Points of comparison for the six approaches

Medical/biological

- Focuses on biological processes and not on emotions, cognition or behaviour
- Looks at biological functioning for reasons and solutions, e.g. drug therapies/surgery
- A scientific approach

Psychodynamic

- Focuses on first 5 years' experiences and on emotional problems caused by repression of thoughts into the unconscious — where energy is used up keeping them unconscious
- Deterministic like a medical model, but looks to talking cures rather than drugs
- Aims to be scientific, but some say it is idiographic

Behavioural

- Focuses on behaviour, which is measurable and testable
- We can treat behaviour and change it — so problems can be solved
- Ignores other issues — reinforcement patterns and associations must be changed if there are problems
- A scientific approach

Cognitive

- Thought processes cause problems when they are negative
- Change our thinking and cure some problems
- Scientific even though individualistic to an extent

Humanistic

- We all are programmed to self-actualise, and problems with this will cause mental health problems
- Very idiographic/individualistic — more so than the others

Social

- Sees the need to look at social factors that both cause mental disorders (or contribute to them) and can help in treatments
- Learning approach emphasises environment too, and psychodynamic approach focuses on early upbringing

> **Tip**
>
> You can be asked to compare any of the six approaches. Expect to be asked to compare any two (and these can be a named two). This is done briefly for you in Tables 2 and 3, but you should prepare your own answers too. Note that what you learn here will be useful for Unit 6.

Specific mental disorders

For this part of the clinical psychology application, you must study two of the following: eating disorders, anxiety disorders, mood disorders and schizophrenia. The last two have been chosen for study here, partly because they are useful in illustrating the treatments and therapies outlined in the previous section. If you have studied one or both of the other two disorders, then you might consider revising from your own notes rather than trying to master any new material.

Schizophrenia

Main symptoms and features of schizophrenia

Schizophrenia is a psychosis, which means that the individual does not have the grip on reality that someone suffering from a neurosis has. Symptoms of schizophrenia include hallucinations, thought disorders, language disturbances and inappropriate feelings (or flattening of feelings).

There are five different types of schizophrenia (as listed in the summary below). The different types are characterised by different symptoms. For example, catatonic schizophrenia involves immobility or excessive motor activity (or some rigidity of posture), whereas these might not occur in other sorts of schizophrenia. Indeed, the diagnosis of the type of schizophrenia is made by reference to such symptoms, so it is hard to make a list of symptoms of schizophrenia without referring to the different types.

Around 1% of the population has schizophrenia and this statistic is more or less the same across all cultures. This might suggest an element of genetic cause — if it were environmental, one might expect different levels of schizophrenia in different cultures.

There are some gender differences (again possibly suggesting a genetic cause). Men tend to exhibit symptoms sooner, usually between 14 and 25 years old, whereas women show symptoms between about 24 and 35 years old.

> **Evaluation**
>
> ± With five types of an illness, and many varying symptoms that in some ways contradict (e.g. withdrawal versus excessive excitability, or rigidity of posture versus excessive movement), it might be suggested that 'schizophrenia' is only a term used to cover a range of 'odd' or abnormal behaviours. Perhaps it is not 'one thing' at all. In this case it would not have one cause either.
>
> ± Some of the above information suggests that there is a genetic element to schizophrenia. This would be useful evidence if you were discussing the nature/nurture debate. More about this is outlined on pp. 48–53. If it is argued that there are many types of schizophrenia, probably some types or some parts of it are inherited and other parts or types come about through environmental pressures.

Summary

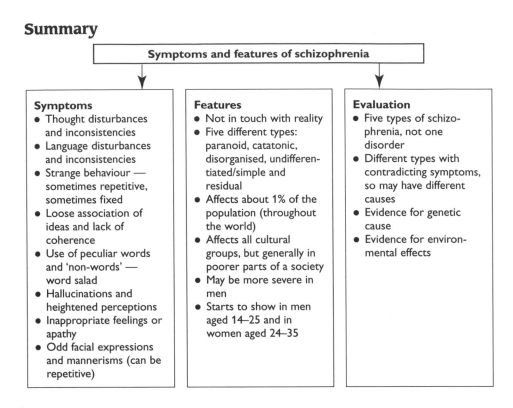

Symptoms and features of schizophrenia		

Symptoms
- Thought disturbances and inconsistencies
- Language disturbances and inconsistencies
- Strange behaviour — sometimes repetitive, sometimes fixed
- Loose association of ideas and lack of coherence
- Use of peculiar words and 'non-words' — word salad
- Hallucinations and heightened perceptions
- Inappropriate feelings or apathy
- Odd facial expressions and mannerisms (can be repetitive)

Features
- Not in touch with reality
- Five different types: paranoid, catatonic, disorganised, undifferentiated/simple and residual
- Affects about 1% of the population (throughout the world)
- Affects all cultural groups, but generally in poorer parts of a society
- May be more severe in men
- Starts to show in men aged 14–25 and in women aged 24–35

Evaluation
- Five types of schizophrenia, not one disorder
- Different types with contradicting symptoms, so may have different causes
- Evidence for genetic cause
- Evidence for environmental effects

Tip

You might be asked about symptoms or features or both. You can use these terms more or less interchangeably, but note that there are some differences in what each term means. Features are anything that applies to schizophrenia, e.g. 1% of the population is likely to be diagnosed as having it. Symptoms are characteristics that are displayed by those diagnosed with it.

Positive/negative symptoms

Sometimes symptoms of schizophrenia are split into positive and negative ones. Positive symptoms are when someone with schizophrenia exhibits a behaviour that is not 'normal'. Negative symptoms are when a schizophrenic fails to exhibit a 'normal' behaviour.

Positive symptoms
Disorganised speech including loose association/derailment
Loose association is when someone changes from one topic to another during speech, with no connection between the topics. For example, 'It's all part of the family, you know, those who are in and the ones who never get to see the words' (Kendall and Hammen, 1995).

Evaluation

– Andreason (1979) says that other disorders, such as mania, can also show loose associations and that not all of those with schizophrenia have disorganised speech.

Delusions

Delusions are thoughts that most of society would disagree with, or are misinterpretations of reality, e.g. the belief that others are plotting against you, and can hear your private conversations to gather evidence for a plot to discredit you. Delusions are found in 50% of schizophrenic patients, but also in mania and delusional depression.

There are several different types of delusion. People with:
- **somatic passivity** think they receive bodily sensations from another agency
- **thought insertion** think that thoughts that are not their own are placed in their mind
- **thought broadcast** think their thoughts are broadcast so that others can hear them
- **thought withdrawal** think that their thoughts are being stolen
- **made feelings** think that others make their feelings and interpretations for them
- **made volitional acts** think that they do not control their actions
- **made impulses** think they are not controlling their impulses

Hallucinations

The world seems unreal, the body seems depersonalised and the person has odd sensations such as burning or numbness. Individuals can experience acute perceptions, such as very bright light or clear colours. On the other hand, they can experience a flattening or dullness.

Hallucinations are sensory experiences in the absence of any stimulation from the environment and involve mainly auditory perceptions (sounds). In schizophrenia, hallucinations often involve hearing voices arguing or voices commenting.

Negative symptoms

Avolition/apathy

This is characterised by a lack of energy and an absence of interest, even in routine. For example, a person may not brush his/her hair and may have dishevelled clothing.

Alogia

This refers to negative thought disorder. There is poverty of speech, and also poor content of speech, giving little information.

Anhedonia

This is an inability to experience pleasure. There is a lack of interest in recreational activities and no relationships are formed.

Flat affect

This means that an individual exhibits no emotions. It is found in 66% of schizophrenics, according to an International Pilot Study of Schizophrenia (IPSS) survey in 1974.

± The person may experience emotions inside, but not show these. Kring (1990) compared schizophrenics with flat affect with normal participants when watching a film, and the former showed no emotions. However, when asked about the film afterwards, the individuals with flat affect reported the same emotions — they just had not shown them.

Other symptoms
The following symptoms are neither positive nor negative.

Catatonia
This refers to a tendency to adopt strange facial expressions or to gesture repeatedly. Some people move much more than usual and show excited movements. Others are immobile and unusual positions are adopted for quite a long time.

Inappropriate affect
This is when someone shows the wrong emotional responses to a situation.

Possible causes of schizophrenia
There is no single accepted explanation for what we diagnose as schizophrenia. Different approaches explain schizophrenia in different ways.

Tip

Some explanations of schizophrenia were given when different approaches to mental disorders were outlined and evaluated in the previous section. Before reading on, make a brief list of the six approaches dealt with and note down what explanation for schizophrenia you think each might give. Check your list against Box 1 on p. 53.

Biological factors
Genetic
Family and twin studies suggest that there is an element of heritability regarding schizophrenia.

Twin studies:
- Gottesman (1991) found that close relatives have a risk factor of 46% (this means that if one person has schizophrenia, there is a 46% chance of a close relative developing schizophrenia). Gottesman also found that identical (MZ) twins have a 48% risk factor (if one twin has it, there is a 48% likelihood that the other one will). Non-identical (DZ) twins have a 17% risk factor. The likelihood of developing schizophrenia for the whole population is 1%, so these findings strongly suggest a genetic factor.
- Torrey (1992) found lower figures than Gottesman's, but still 28% for identical twins and 6% for non-identical twins, so higher than the 1%.
- McGue (1992) found a risk factor of 40% for identical twins.

Adoption studies:
- The environment of an adopted child is not shared with the biological family, so if the biological family likelihood of developing schizophrenia reflects the likelihood of the adopted child doing so, then it would seem that this is due to genes and not to environment.
- It is found that an adopted child who develops schizophrenia is likely to have a biological parent with schizophrenia.
- An adopted child raised in a (non-biological) family where a member has schizophrenia is not so likely to develop it.
- Thus it seems that biological background, rather than an environment in which schizophrenia is present, leads to an individual developing schizophrenia.

Evaluation

+ All three twin studies mentioned above found more than the 1% expected — this is quite strong evidence for a genetic cause (nature).
+ The biological link with schizophrenia in families compared with the lack of environmental link — using evidence from adoption studies — is quite compelling evidence.
− The three different twin studies found different figures, which means evidence must be questioned.
− In the twin studies, twins (and relatives to an extent) share environment as well as genes, so the above percentages might be evidence that schizophrenia is environmentally caused (nurture).
− Schizophrenia may be linked to more than one gene, so it is hard to pin down a genetic cause.
− There seems to be more than one type of schizophrenia, so there may be more than one cause.
− If it was wholly caused by genetics, one MZ twin should automatically develop schizophrenia if the other one does, because MZ twins share 100% of their genes. However, this is not the case — even the highest estimate is just under 50%.

Neurochemical

Neurochemical medication seems to help in the relief of the symptoms of schizophrenia. This suggests that a neurotransmitter is the problem, or that there might be problems with synaptic transmission. Phenothiazine drugs reduce symptoms of schizophrenia and block dopamine receptors, so schizophrenia may be due to excess dopamine — a neurotransmitter (and chemical). This is the dopamine hypothesis. Drugs that increase dopamine activity (such as amphetamine) make the symptoms worse, which is added evidence for a neurochemical cause.

Evaluation

+ Given the evidence, it is tempting to link the two factors (excess dopamine with schizophrenia).

+ If medication helps, and medication changes the neurochemical pattern, then it is tempting to think that the pattern caused the problem.

– Not all those with schizophrenia respond to drug treatment, so it seems that not all incidents of schizophrenia are caused by excess dopamine.

– Drugs work with some symptoms but not all — again suggesting that excess dopamine, even if part of the story for some, is not the whole story. More research is needed.

– The excess dopamine may be produced in response to the schizophrenia; it may not be a cause of it.

Neurological

This explanation looks at brain structure itself. Scanning has helped by imaging the brains of schizophrenics. It is possible that those with schizophrenia have enlarged ventricles, or they could have reduced areas in the prefrontal cortex (Shenton et al., 1992). Cognitive functioning seems to be impaired in those with schizophrenia, which may suggest that brain abnormalities like these cause it.

Evaluation

+ When something is found in quite a few sufferers of the same symptoms/disease, it is tempting to think that there is a causal link — or at least that this is an important finding.

+ The evidence for this link is quite strong.

– Having schizophrenia may cause the brain difference, not the other way around.

– Not all those with schizophrenia have enlarged ventricles. This could mean that there is more than one kind of schizophrenia or that the enlargement is not connected.

– Those with enlarged ventricles are mainly those who have problems with cognitive functioning and those for whom medication does not work. This could suggest either that enlarged ventricles is not a cause or that schizophrenia is not 'one thing'.

Conclusion

The evidence suggests that there is at least some role for biological factors. However, as there is no evidence that biological causes are the whole story (even MZ twins only have just under a 50% likelihood of both having schizophrenia — less according to some studies) there is plenty of room for environmental causes.

Social factors

Labelling theory

Scheff (1966) said that schizophrenia is a learned social role. Individuals are labelled as having schizophrenia and then fulfil the role. The label leads to people acting as they think they should act and also affects how others react to them. Without the label, there would not be the behaviour, or at least the behaviour leading to the diagnosis would have been there, but not stabilised by the diagnosis. Without the diagnosis, this inappropriate behaviour would be more likely to have been temporary.

Scheff thinks that breaking social norms is quite common, but only some are caught and then diagnosed as mentally ill. Once the diagnosis has taken place, labelling determines behaviour in the way outlined above.

Evaluation

- There needs to be more evidence that giving someone the label 'mentally ill' has such a strong effect.
- Schizophrenic behaviour is more than some breaking of social norms. Murphy (1976) found that even in two different cultures with different norms there were very similar ideas about what schizophrenia was.
- Labelling is not really accepted as an explanation of schizophrenia itself, although it could be a factor in the behaviour of schizophrenics. One reason is that the behaviour of some schizophrenics, such as those with catatonia, is clearly not the result of obeying social rules.

The effect of social class

General life stresses can precipitate a relapse, so perhaps they are a cause of schizophrenia. Social class seems to be linked to the incidence of schizophrenia. These are two social factors that could be considered when looking at causes.

Sociogenic hypothesis — the highest rate of schizophrenia is in central city areas, which are inhabited by the lowest socioeconomic class (Srole et al., 1962). In these areas, the incidence of schizophrenia can be as much as double normal levels, so we can ask whether social class is in some way a cause of schizophrenia. The sociogenic hypothesis suggests that stress from a low level of education, with poor rewards and opportunities, can lead to schizophrenia.

Social selection theory suggests that it is not that class causes schizophrenia but that those with the illness drift downwards in terms of class. They may earn less because of cognitive and motivational difficulties.

Evaluation

± Some studies, such as Schwartz's (1946), show that schizophrenics are downwardly mobile, but other studies (e.g. Dunham, 1965) show that they are not. One way of testing this is to see if fathers of those with schizophrenia are lower class. Social class is often determined by the father's status and this would show that schizophrenics were members of the lower classes rather than arriving there by downward mobility. If fathers are lower class, this supports the sociogenic hypothesis. Studies tend to show that fathers of schizophrenics are lower class, but they also show that those with schizophrenia earn less and become downwardly mobile — so they support both hypotheses.

± Dohrenwend et al. (1992) looked at ethnic minorities. Because of prejudice and discrimination, and resultant stress, one would expect ethnic minority groups to have more incidents of schizophrenia across all classes. However, the rates are higher in lower-class groups, which seems to be evidence of social selection, not the sociogenic hypothesis.

Psychological factors

Psychodynamic explanations

Freud dealt with neuroses; schizophrenia is a psychosis. Psychodynamic theory does not deal directly with schizophrenia, but does consider reasons for disordered personalities. It suggests that schizophrenics have regressed to a state of narcissism, and that they are in the oral stage with the id in control. The ego is not developed, so reality testing does not take place. Schizophrenics, therefore, form no attachment to the world and have regressed. This could be caused by intense id impulses. These impulses could be sexual, as Freud might have said, or could be aggressive, as would be more accepted now. If the ego is relatively strong, neuroses may develop, but not schizophrenia. It is when the ego is weak that regression will take place.

Evaluation

– Evidence is weak. Cognitive deficits in schizophrenia may point to lack of ego, but very little research has been done. This explanation is not really an accepted one.

The schizophrenogenic mother: the double-bind theory

The schizophrenogenic mother is said to be cold, dominant and conflict-inducing (Fromm-Reichmann, 1948) and if there is this sort of relationship between mother and son, schizophrenia can result. These mothers are rejecting, overprotective, self-sacrificing, rigid, moralistic about sex and fear intimacy. Bateson et al. (1956) explains how the processes involved in this sort of mothering lead to schizophrenia, and presents the double-bind theory.

Double-bind situations include:

- an intense relationship with someone else, where it is important for communication to be clearly understood, as the relationship is so intense
- a relationship with a person who gives out two messages when making a statement, and the two messages contradict (e.g. saying he/she loves someone and then pulling away)
- an individual not having the power to comment on the conflicting messages he/she is being subjected to (i.e. choosing to ignore them or withdraw)

An example of such a situation is when a son feels he needs to show his mother that he loves her (she wants that) but if this is demonstrated with a hug, for example, the mother pulls away, so it is important for him not to demonstrate affection. Families which include a schizophrenic family member do show some atypical communication patterns, which is evidence for this theory.

Evaluation

+ Norton (1982) studied adolescent behaviour patterns and recorded communication and interaction patterns. It was later found that those who developed schizophrenia were from those families that had had communication difficulties. This is evidence for the double-bind hypothesis.

– Miklowitz (1985), however, shows that there are communication difficulties in families where a member has mania, so the communication problems might be a factor in schizophrenia rather than a single cause.

- It could be that having someone with schizophrenia in the family causes unfocused communication patterns, rather than the other way around.

Genetics and the environment

Tienari et al. (1987) carried out studies in Finland. They studied the environment of adopted children, some of whom had mothers with schizophrenia and some of whom did not. The more problematic the environment, the more severe problems the children of schizophrenics had. A problematic environment did not, however, lead to problems in adopted children without a schizophrenic mother. It seems, therefore, that an element of genetic predisposition, as well as environmental influences, leads to schizophrenia.

Box 1 Six approaches and possible explanations for schizophrenia

Medical/biological
Genes — twin studies show a family link, as do adoption studies. Children of schizophrenics who are adopted and not in the 'schizophrenic' environment are still more likely to develop it.

Neurochemical problems (e.g. excess dopamine) could be a cause.

Differences or problems with brain structure (e.g. enlarged ventricles) might also be a cause.

Psychodynamic
Schizophrenia could be caused by regression to an 'id' state and at the same time having a weak ego. However, there is little evidence for this.

Behavioural and other psychological explanations
Adopted children of schizophrenic mothers suffer more from a problematic environment than do adopted children with no schizophrenic mother.

Environment affects the development of schizophrenia, but so do genes.

The double-bind theory and examination of the schizophrenogenic mother suggest that poor communication patterns in families might lead to schizophrenia, but having someone with schizophrenia in the family might lead to poor communication patterns.

Cognitive
Apart from the double-bind theory and the general idea that there is faulty thinking involved, the cognitive approach does not offer an explanation, so it is not a helpful approach to use. The double-bind explanation is included in the behavioural approach which comes under 'other psychological explanations'.

Humanistic
Apart from claiming that mental illness would develop from the lack of an opportunity to self-actualise, the humanistic approach does not offer an explanation for schizophrenia, so it is not a helpful one to use.

Social
Labelling someone as having schizophrenia (due to some breaking of social norms) can lead to that person behaving in a schizophrenic manner.

The sociogenic hypothesis suggests that lower classes suffer more from schizophrenia for class reasons, but the social selection hypothesis suggests that it is the schizophrenia that leads to downward mobility and explains the higher incidence in lower classes.

Mood disorders (including unipolar and bipolar)

Two main mood disorders are dealt with here: unipolar disorder (depression) and bipolar disorder (manic depression and mania).

> **Tip**
>
> Note that 'mood disorder' itself is not *one* mental disorder, so when asked for 'one mental disorder you have studied' you need to focus on either unipolar or bipolar disorder. (The same applies to eating disorders, which are not *one* mental disorder, so focus on either anorexia or bulimia.)

Main symptoms of mood disorders

Unipolar disorder (major depression)

Depression may be associated with other psychological disorders such as agoraphobia or alcoholism, but here it is dealt with as a main diagnosis. Major depression disorders include:

- psychotic depression (departure from reality)
- melancholic depression (physical symptoms)
- seasonal affective disorder (due to seasonal problems, such as lack of daylight)

Symptoms include feelings of worthlessness and hopelessness, loss of sleep and appetite, guilt, sadness and loss of interest and pleasure in usual activities. For some sufferers, paying attention is difficult and conversation can be hard. Others find it hard to switch off and cannot sit still. Some develop hypochondria.

Symptoms change with age. Depression in children can mean aggression and a lot of activity, whereas in adolescents it is often characterised by antisocial behaviour and feelings of being misunderstood. In older adults, it leads to memory problems and distractibility. Phases of depression can last for up to 6 months.

When using the *DSM* for diagnosis, only some of these symptoms have to be present for the diagnosis to be made. For there to be a diagnosis of unipolar disorder, there must be mood disturbances, loss of (or too much) sleep, loss (or gain) of weight, loss (or gain) of appetite and a disturbed activity level. *DSM-IV* says that there must be five symptoms from the list and that these must last for at least 2 weeks. Depressed mood and loss of pleasure or interest must be two of these five symptoms.

Unipolar depression tends to start between the ages of 40 and 50, and is more common in women and lower socioeconomic groups.

Bipolar disorder (manic depression)

Someone diagnosed with bipolar disorder can experience manic phases as well as depression. In some people, the bouts of depression and mania alternate. Symptoms of mania include hyperactivity, distractibility, flights of ideas, unfounded emotional highs, purposeless activity and grandiose plans. Mania is characterised by the switching of attention from one thing to another and there can be an endless stream of comment about what is being attended to. The person speaking can switch from topic to topic and become angry if someone intervenes.

Bipolar disorder can seriously affect functioning. The age of onset tends to be around 30 and it occurs less than major depression (unipolar). Goodwin and Jamison (1990) point out that the depression phase is more common than the euphoric/manic one. If the person only suffers from mania, it is still called bipolar disorder as there are similar problems for the individual.

Unipolar vs bipolar

Unipolar disorder leads to more agitation. It also tends to cause problems with sleeping, whereas in bipolar disorder the person tends to sleep more when depressed. The average age of onset is different: 30 for bipolar, yet between 40 and 50 for major depression. Unipolar is found more in women, but bipolar is equal between the sexes. Unipolar disorder tends to be treated with tricyclic drugs, whereas bipolar disorder tends to be treated with lithium.

Possible causes of mood disorders

There is no single accepted explanation for what we diagnose as mood disorders. There are many different disorders, so there is not going to be one cause. The various approaches explain mood disorders in different ways.

> **Tip**
>
> Some explanations of mood disorders were given when different approaches to mental disorders were outlined and evaluated (pp. 29–30 and p. 33). Before reading on, make a quick list of the six approaches dealt with and note down what explanation for mood disorders you think they might give. It would help to focus on depression here. Check your list against Box 2 on p. 61.

Physiological (biological) factors
Genetic

If someone has bipolar disorder, there is a 10–20% chance that a first-degree relative will develop a mood disorder too, which is higher than the rate for the general population. This suggests a genetic component or cause. However, although there is this high link for mood disorders in relatives of those with a bipolar disorder, the mood disorder is often unipolar rather than bipolar.

Allen (1976) looked at twins and found that the concordance rate for bipolar disorder in MZ twins was 72%, which is very high indeed. Remember, this means that if one identical twin has bipolar disorder, there is a 72% likelihood that the other twin has a mood disorder too. This research suggests a genetic element (though note that identical twins share a lot of their environment and interactions, and might model on each other too). Allen also found a 14% concordance rate for DZ twins (who also share interactions and environment), which again suggests a genetic cause for bipolar disorder.

In unipolar disorders, genes do not play as strong a role as in bipolar disorders. However, as outlined above, if there is a bipolar disorder in the family, there is quite a strong chance of a first-degree relative developing a mood disorder, which is often unipolar. This suggests that unipolar disorder could be genetic and linked to bipolar disorder.

- Andreason et al. (1987) points out that there is more risk of unipolar disorder developing in families with bipolar disorder than in families with unipolar disorder.
- Allen (1976) suggests a concordance rate of 40% for MZ twins and 11% for DZ twins, which suggests a genetic component for unipolar disorder, but not as strong as that for bipolar disorder.
- Adoption studies support the claim that genes are involved in depression. For example, Cadoret (1978) found that there were more mood disorders in adopted children where one of the biological parents had a mood disorder.

Evaluation

+ Adoption and twin studies seem to show that there is at least some genetic component in depression, and more so for bipolar depression.
− Although we can draw conclusions about genes from twin studies, we must not overlook the very similar environments and interactions that twins share. Even if we say that the rates for MZ twins are always higher than for DZ and that this proves the genetic element, we could counter this by claiming that there are closer similarities in the environments and treatments experienced by MZ twins.
− If depression were entirely genetic, both MZ twins would always develop a mood disorder, and this is not the case.

Neurochemical

There is evidence to suggest that low levels of norepinephrine can cause depression and high levels can cause mania. This suggests that there is a biological basis for mood disorders. Another neurotransmitter that might be involved is serotonin. Serotonin is often involved in neural activity involving other neurotransmitters. If serotonin levels are low, this could lead to problems in other neural activity and consequently depression or mania.

Evidence comes from the success of tricyclic drugs and monamine oxidase inhibitors in alleviating depression. Tricyclic drugs interfere with the reuptake of norepinephrine and serotonin. This suggests a role for these neurotransmitters in causing depression, because the lack of reuptake might mean more of them at the synapse. Monoamine oxidase inhibitors stop the enzyme monoamine oxidase from deactivating neurotransmitters. This will increase levels of serotonin and norepinephrine.

Another piece of evidence is that reserpine, which is prescribed to calm those with schizophrenia, led to some patients developing depression. Reserpine lowers levels of serotonin and norepinephrine, and this again is evidence that low levels of these neurotransmitters might cause depression. Bunney et al. (1970) found decreased levels of norepinephrine in the urine of sufferers of bipolar disorder, when these sufferers moved to the depressed phase. This too strengthens claims for the role of neurotransmitters. Bunney et al. (1972) added to this evidence when they found increased levels of the two neurotransmitters as the sufferer moved to the manic stage.

Evaluation

+ All the above evidence points to the role of these two neurotransmitters in both unipolar and bipolar disorders.
+ Shopsin et al. (1976) found that a drug that suppresses the synthesis of serotonin reduces the effect of drugs given for depression. If serotonin is not synthesised (not present), then antidepressant drugs are not as effective. Perhaps the drugs cannot increase levels of serotonin by preventing reuptake, as serotonin is not there in the first place. This also suggests that low levels of serotonin could be a cause of depression, as claimed above.
− It could be that the mood disorder led to the change in level of serotonin rather than the level causing the mood disorder.
− As research continues, the above findings are being contradicted. Tricyclics and monoamine oxidase inhibitors do seem to increase levels of norepinephrine and serotonin at first, but after a few days the norepinephrine levels go back to normal. As it takes more than a week for tricyclics and monoamine oxidase inhibitors to work, and as by this time the neurotransmitter levels are back to normal, the idea that the low levels of these two neurotransmitters cause depression must be challenged.
− Other antidepressant drugs work, but not by increasing levels of these two neurotransmitters (Cole, 1986).
− Much of the research comes from animal studies and we must take care when generalising findings from animal studies to humans.

Neuroendocrine

The limbic area of the brain affects the hypothalamus and is linked to emotions. The hypothalamus controls endocrine glands and the secretion of hormones. The hypothalamic-pituitary-adrenal (HPA) axis is thought to be important in depression.

Cortisol is an adrenocortical hormone and levels are high in those with depression. The suppression of cortisol might not take place and this might cause the depression. In Cushing's syndrome, there is oversecretion of cortisol and the individual then suffers from depression. It may be that the high levels of cortisol lower the density of serotonin receptors — thus linking this explanation to the role of neurotransmitters.

Disorders of thyroid function are found in those with bipolar disorder, and thyroid hormones can lead these patients to experience a bout of mania. The hypothalamic-pituitary-thyroid system, as well as the HPA system, seems to be implicated in bipolar disorder.

+ Evidence suggests that there are changes in hormonal activity in those with mood disorders.
− It is hard to tell whether changes come from the mood disorder or whether the mood disorder is caused by such changes.
− It is not easy to separate the role of the endocrine system and hormones from the role of the central nervous system and neurotransmitters.
− Some of the evidence comes from animal studies. These can be criticised on the grounds that it is difficult to generalise results to humans.

Social factors

Stress might be a cause of depression and is the result of environmental triggers. The psychodynamic approach focuses on loss and how this can lead to depression (outlined on p. 59), but the social approach focuses more on stressful life events than on loss in particular — although loss is part of life stress. Studies of depressed people in hospitals generally show that these people have experienced stressful life events (Hammen, 1991). Not only do stressful life events seem to lead to depression, but they also interfere with recovery (e.g. Billings and Moos, 1985).

However, many people experience negative life events without becoming clinically depressed. It may be that negative thinking patterns and the individual's cognitive approach dictates whether someone becomes depressed or not when faced with stressors. (The cognitive explanation for depression is outlined on pp. 59–60.)

In addition, people require different levels and types of social support. Some people need to be successful; others need close personal relationships. It is, therefore, hard to predict who will become depressed when faced with life stressors and who will not.

Another factor involved in depression is gender — more women become depressed then men. This could be because women face different stressors from men or it could be because the sexes have different coping strategies. For example, women may use more emotion-focusing strategies than men, and emotion focusing is not always the best strategy.

+ Many studies have shown that those hospitalised for depression have experienced stressful life events.
+ Stress does seem to be a factor, not only in leading to depression but also in how quickly a person recovers.
− It can be seen that social factors might lead to depression; however, psychological factors, such as a person's thinking patterns and what they need to feel good, are also involved.
− It is hard to separate social factors from psychological ones where depression is concerned.

    – Probably a better explanation is found in diathesis–stress models. There are psychological diatheses, such as loss in early childhood or cognitive vulnerability, and there are biological diatheses, such as genetic predisposition or the effect of seasonal patterns of day and night. Alongside these diatheses there are stress factors from society and the environment, and these should all be taken into account when looking at causes of depression.

Psychological factors

> **Tip**
>
> Recall the main points of the psychodynamic approach, especially the description of the personality as being id, ego and superego. This will help in understanding the psychodynamic theory of depression.

The psychodynamic theory of depression

Two parts of the psychodynamic theory are important here. First, if fixated at the oral stage, people may be dependent on others for their self-esteem. Second, if people experience loss in childhood they incorporate the lost person — they become them. According to the idea of people having negative feelings towards people they love, these individuals will then both love and have negative feelings towards themselves, through incorporating the person they have lost. There is also guilt about the one they have lost. Normally there would be mourning and the feelings would be worked through, but in someone who is very dependent (orally fixated) the self-hate feelings can be dominant and depression can develop.

> **Evaluation**
>
> + Society has accepted some of Freud's explanations — such as the dependency of the oral character — and these help to explain depression.
> + It does seem to be the case that depression is brought on by stressful life events and these often involve loss.
> – People become depressed without losing someone and we would need to say that the loss was symbolic rather than real — such as suffering a rejection. Symbols of loss could, perhaps, apply to anyone.
> – Beck and Ward (1961) looked at the dreams of depressed people and found thoughts of love and failure but no thoughts of anger and hating, so this does not support the psychodynamic explanation.

Cognitive theory of depression

Depression is often characterised by negative thoughts, feelings of helplessness and irrational beliefs. Beck (1967, 1987) thought depression arose from negative interpretations of events. Individuals who become depressed develop negative schemata. This can be for reasons such as rejection by peers, loss of a parent, or criticism from teachers. These schemata are then triggered by new situations. There are also cognitive biases, such as individuals thinking they will fail or feeling responsible for problems. There is a triad of negative views — of the self, the world and the future.

According to Davison and Neale (1994), cognitive biases include:

- **arbitrary inference** — feeling worthless, although there is no evidence (e.g. simply because it is raining)
- **selective abstraction** — feeling worthless because of a problem even though many others are involved in it too (e.g. at work)
- **overgeneralisation** — taking a trivial event and drawing a wide conclusion about worthlessness (e.g. one wrong answer in a test)
- **magnification** and **minimisation** — magnification is when a small event is magnified and a feeling of worthlessness ensues (e.g. a scratch on the car means the car is ruined) and minimisation is when a person feels worthless even when they have just done something good

Beck thought that illogical thoughts and judgements can be changed by the individual.

Evaluation

+ Beck (1967) and White et al. (1992) showed that depressed people do have cognitive biases such as those outlined by Davidson and Neale.
+ After treatment, biased thinking seems to disappear, according to Simons et al. (1984).
− Other studies, such as Dykman et al. (1991), have not found such biases. Depressed people do not seem to have a distorted perception of their own abilities. Perhaps they do focus on the negative parts of events but they do perceive them accurately, which is a slightly different explanation.
− Perhaps the mood (being depressed) is what distorts perceptions, rather than the distorted perceptions causing the mood. Lewinsohn et al. (1981) found negative thinking did not come before depression, which suggests that depression causes the cognitive biases, not the other way around.

Learning theory and learned helplessness as causes of depression

If people have learned by past experiences that they can do nothing about certain things, then they might become passive and have feelings of lack of control over their lives. This can cause depression. Seligman (1974) found that when dogs were given electric shocks they could not avoid, they did not try to escape when later the shocks became avoidable. They had learned helplessness. They did escape eventually, but learned the avoidance response much more slowly than did a control group which had not had the training with the unavoidable shocks. The dogs who had learned helplessness (by having unavoidable shocks first) became passive. Depressed people exhibit the same symptoms of helplessness and passivity. In addition, the appetite of the dogs suffered (as did their weight), just as in depressed humans.

Evaluation

+ Studies (e.g. Roth and Kubal, 1975) have shown that when participants are faced with an inescapable noise or some unsolvable problem, later, when they can avoid the noise or do the problem, they do not try to do so. This supports Seligman's findings with dogs.

- Some studies, such as that by Wortman and Brehm (1975), have found that helplessness actually improves later performance, which goes against Seligman's findings.
- It is thought that it is not so much that people feel helpless as that they blame themselves. Attribution, rather than learned helplessness, seems to be a key element.

Box 2 Six approaches and possible explanations for mood disorders

Medical/biological

Genes seem to play a part — more so for bipolar than unipolar (there is a 72% link for MZ twins for bipolar and a 40% link for MZ twins for unipolar). A relative of someone with bipolar is more likely to develop a mood disorder than the general population, but is more likely to develop unipolar than bipolar (which suggests a link between the two).

Neurotransmitters also might play a role — especially serotonin and norepinephrine, low levels of which might give depression while high levels might give mania. There is quite a lot of evidence for this, but also some against. The mood disorder might change levels of the chemicals and not the other way around.

The hypothalamic-pituitary-adrenal axis is important — oversecretion of cortisol might cause depression.

Psychodynamic

If someone is orally fixated, they are dependent on others for their self-esteem. If they experience loss (real or symbolic), then they incorporate the lost person into themselves, and both love the person and hate them (and feel guilty about them). These feelings are not resolved by a period of mourning in those who are orally fixated, and the feelings mean they develop depression.

Behavioural

Learned helplessness may account for depression. If dogs cannot avoid a shock, when later they can avoid it they don't — or at least they take longer to learn that they can avoid it than does a control group (Seligman, 1974). Studies with people have shown, for example, that if at first participants cannot escape a noise, when later they can avoid it they don't try to — they are passive. The dogs had problems with appetite and weight just as depressed people do.

Cognitive

Cognitive biases and negative thinking might lead to depression, according to Beck (1987). Treatment of these biases and distorted perceptions does seem to improve depression, but depression might cause the negative thoughts and not the other way around.

Humanistic

The humanistic approach does not offer an explanation of mood disorders directly, although any barrier to self-actualisation is likely to lead to low self-esteem and could lead to depression.

Social

Stressful life events can lead to a diagnosis of clinical depression. Those hospitalised for depression do seem to have experienced such events. However, there are those who do not suffer from depression yet still experience stressful lives. Psychological factors, such as thinking patterns, and social conditions, such as level and type of support, also seem to be important.

Questions
&
Answers

The questions that follow are presented in three sections, one for each area of the clinical psychology specification:

- Defining and classification
- Approaches and therapies
- Specific mental disorders

Choose one area of the specification and revise the material using this unit guide. Work through the questions for your chosen area, answering them yourself without reading the advice on how to answer the question and without reading the answers given. Then mark your own answers, and read through the advice on what is required. Did you interpret the question successfully? Read through the answers given and note where the marks are awarded. Finally, read through the examiner's comments to see what full answers should include.

Examiner's comments

All questions and answers are followed by examiner's comments. These are preceded by the icon *e*. They indicate where credit is due and point out areas for improvement, specific problems and common errors such as poor time management, lack of clarity, weak or non-existent development, irrelevance, misinterpretation of the question and mistaken meanings of terms.

Defining and classification

(1) Describe the *DSM* approach to classifying mental disorders.   (4 marks, AO1)
(2) Explain how issues of reliability affect diagnosis.   (4 marks, AO2)
(3) Explain how issues of validity affect diagnosis.   (4 marks, AO2)
(4) Explain how cultural issues affect diagnosis.   (4 marks, AO2)
(5) Outline *one* definition of abnormality.   (2 marks, AO1)
(6) Explain the problems of using this definition.   (5 marks, AO2)
(7) Compare and contrast *two* definitions of abnormality.   (12 marks, essay)

 (1) There are different versions of *DSM*; you should describe *DSM-IV* as it is the most recent. 1 mark can be gained for each point made and further marks can be earned for any points that are developed. A list of the five axes would gain you a maximum of 2 marks if the list is not expanded upon.

(2) 1 mark is available for saying what reliability is in this context — don't just say what reliability is in a methodological sense. You need to give some evidence to show whether diagnosis has been reliable or not in different studies, and what the result of this reliability or lack of it has been. Make sure you say enough for 4 marks and include some evaluation (AO2).

(3) 1 mark is available for saying what validity is in this context — don't just say what validity is in a methodological sense. You need to give evidence to show whether diagnoses have been valid or not. Make sure you say enough for 4 marks and include some evaluation (AO2).

(4) You need to use evidence from studies that show that diagnosis can be biased due to cultural factors. You can give examples of culture-bound syndromes but only if you focus clearly on their effect on diagnosis. Make sure you say enough for 4 marks and include some evaluation (AO2).

(5) 1 mark is for knowing one definition of abnormality and another mark is for saying more about it.

(6) Focus on problems rather than strengths. To earn full marks you could either make five separate points, or make two or three points which you elaborate upon.

(7) In this essay question, 2 marks are for clarity and communication and 2 marks are for balance and breadth. This leaves 4 AO1 marks and 4 AO2 marks. You need to describe two definitions of abnormality and then make a few points about where they are similar and where they are different.

■ ■ ■

Answers

(1) *DSM-IV* classifies mental disorders from symptoms and characteristics. It has five axes to create a full picture of the patient. ✓ The axes are: clinical disorders, personality disorders and mental retardation, general medical conditions, psychosocial and environmental problems, and the global assessment of functioning. ✓✓ The last one is a scale that takes into account how the person is functioning, for example in work and social relationships. The psychiatrist takes all the axes into account rather than diagnosing from just one of them. ✓

> *e* This answer earns all 4 marks. Saying that there are five axes gains 1 mark and saying what these are gains a further 2 marks, as the last one is expanded upon a little. The final comment, that more than one aspect is taken into account when diagnosing, earns the final mark.

(2) It is essential that diagnosis is reliable and that diagnoses are consistent. ✓ It has been shown that psychiatrists can differ by up to 50% in their diagnoses. ✓ Cooper et al. (1982) set up the UK and US diagnosis project and this showed that in the USA, schizophrenia was twice as likely to be diagnosed as in the UK. ✓ In the UK, depression and mania were more likely to be diagnosed.

> *e* This answer scores 3 out of 4 marks. Evidence that diagnosis is not reliable is given with two examples. These examples get 1 mark each, but it would have been better if both examples were sourced. The third mark is earned for saying that reliability has to do with consistency, but this point could have been made more clearly. The final mark could have been earned by saying why the different diagnoses are important, and by pointing out that the same person ought to be able to go to the same psychiatrist in any culture and get the same diagnosis if the diagnosis is to be reliable and useful. Alternatively, more examples of problems with reliability could have been given.

(3) For a diagnosis to be valid, it must measure what is it supposed to measure. But a diagnosis will not be valid if it is not reliable. ✓ There are different types of validity here, such as eteological. The most interesting is predictive validity, which looks at the validity of choosing the correct treatment; this is essential. ✓

> *e* This answer scores 2 marks out of 4. The first sentence is rather general and could refer to validity with regard to research methods, but the second sentence helps to clarify it a little. 1 mark is given for these two pieces of information, neither of which is very clear. Etiological validity is not explained (note the incorrect spelling), but predictive validity is outlined in more detail and a good point is made about the importance of getting the treatment right. Another mark is given here. The point needed to be expanded for a further mark to be earned. Another mark could have been achieved by providing an example of how the wrong diagnosis, leading to the wrong treatment, shows the importance of valid diagnoses.

(4) Cultural issues are important in diagnosis. Culture-bound syndromes refer to the idea that some disorders only appear in certain cultures. ✓

e This is a good start, but only 1 mark is given because the answer is far too short. Culture-bound syndromes need to be explained and linked to problems in diagnosis. For example, if disorders are only found in some cultures and in some diagnosis systems, then they will only be diagnosed using those systems. Some-one moving to another culture, for example, would then presumably be diagnosed with a different disorder, possibly with different suggested treatments. This might mean that treatment is not appropriate. More marks could be gained by looking at different cultural interpretations, such as how hearing voices might be interpreted as something spiritual in one culture, but as schizophrenia in another. The answer could also explore how the numbers of diagnoses of schiz-ophrenia among different cultures are likely to be affected by race (or gender) rather than because there are simply more examples of these disorders in particular cultures.

(5) Statistical deviation from the norm ✓ refers to any behaviour that is unusual or done infrequently. ✓ This can be deviation from the norm at the lower end, for example a very low IQ, and can also mean deviation from the norm at the top end, for example a very high IQ. (✓)

e This is a good answer and there is more than enough material for 2 marks. 1 mark is given for the definition (the use of the correct terminology helps). The other mark is given for explaining what this means and for the example.

(6) There is a problem because although we might accept that having a low IQ is abnormal in a mental health sense, we would probably not accept that having a high IQ is abnormal in that sense. ✓ We would agree that it is abnormal to have a high IQ, but we would not label that person mentally ill. It seems that there is more to defining abnormality in the sense of being mentally ill than just deviating from the norm. People might behave abnormally in the sense of being different and standing out from the crowd, but that does not make them mentally ill. ✓ In addition, differing norms mean that mental illness would vary across cultures. However, it is not likely that mental illnesses would vary that much between countries. ✓ Those from one culture who live in another culture would perhaps frequently act in ways that are against the norm of the country where they are living, because they are acting according to the norms of their own culture, but this does not make them mentally ill. ✓ This is not a very useful definition because it defines abnormality in a literal sense and not what we mean by abnormality when referring to those who have a mental disorder. ✓

e This is a good answer which shows how the full 5 marks can be gained. It only discusses one problem — that something can be abnormal in one sense (being against the norm) but this does not mean that it is abnormal in the sense of mental illness. It then gives different examples of how something can be against the norm but not because of a mental disorder. This is quite thorough and the points are made clearly. The final point, suggesting that there are two meanings here for the term 'abnormal', gains a mark because it summarises what has been said.

(7) Two definitions of abnormality are deviation from a statistical norm and deviation from a social norm. Deviation from a statistical norm means that 'normal' is defined as being what most people do and say, and 'abnormal' refers to any behaviour that most people would not exhibit. The idea is that if there are sufficient people in a sample, most people lie within two standard deviations either side of a mean average — this is normal distribution. ✓✓(AO1) This would take care of about 96% of any population. Using the definition that abnormality is deviation from the statistical norm, then 2% either side of that 96% of the population is abnormal (by definition). If we say that in IQ the standard deviation is around 15, and the mean is 100, this means that 70 is the dividing line for the bottom 2% and 130 is the dividing line for the top 2%. So anyone with an IQ of below 70 or above 130 is defined as abnormal.

If the definition of abnormality is deviation from a social norm, then a different criterion is used, this time looking at what people normally do in a social sense. ✓(AO2) Unlike statistical norms, these norms are measured by what society approves of. Most people do socially acceptable things, and this is 'normal'. ✓(AO1) Once someone does something unacceptable, this is abnormal by this definition. ✓(AO1)

When comparing the two definitions it can be seen that someone with a very high IQ is abnormal given the first definition, and indeed having a high IQ is not a social norm either, so the two definitions are similar. ✓(AO2) However, having a high IQ is not socially unacceptable, so is not abnormal using the second definition. In this way, the two definitions disagree. ✓(AO2) We are more likely to agree that people who are abnormal in the sense of mentally ill are likely to be doing things that are socially unacceptable (such as using disorganised speech in schizophrenia), whereas just being statistically abnormal does not mean someone is mentally ill. In fact, disorders such as depression could almost be said to be statistically quite common and not just found in a small percentage of the population. ✓(AO2)

> ✒ This answer balances descriptions of the two definitions of abnormality with comments about their similarities and differences. It gets the full 2 marks for balance and breadth and there is good use of terms, spelling and grammar, so 2 marks are awarded for clarity and communication too. There is a good depth of description of both definitions, so all 4 AO1 marks are given. 4 AO2 marks are also given as the two definitions are said to be similar in some ways and different in others. This answer scores full marks.

Section 2

Approaches and therapies

(1) Describe *one* therapy derived from the behavioural approach. (4 marks, AO1)

(2) Evaluate the therapy described above using one or more of the following criteria: effectiveness, ethics or limitations. (4 marks, AO2)

(3) Discuss the medical/biological approach to the study of mental disorders. (14 marks, essay)

(4) Compare *two* therapeutic approaches to mental disorders. (12 marks, essay)

(5) Describe recent developments in social approaches to mental disorders. (6 marks, AO1)

(6) Discuss the humanistic approach to the study of mental disorders. (12 marks, essay)

(1) 1 mark is for naming the therapy; 3 further marks are for describing it. Obviously, the chosen therapy must come from the behavioural approach.

(2) The answer to this question must refer to the therapy chosen in question 1. Note that you can talk about the effectiveness of the therapy, the ethics of it, and/or its limitations. To earn full marks, you can either say four things in evaluation, or make two evaluation points and expand upon them.

(3) This is an essay question, so there will be 2 marks for clarity and communication and 2 marks for balance and breadth. To demonstrate balance and breadth you need to describe the material and then evaluate it, focusing on AO1 and AO2 equally. There are 5 AO1 marks and 5 AO2 marks.

(4) For this question, you can choose any two therapeutic approaches to mental disorders from the six listed in the specification. Choose two that you can compare — often a good way of doing this it to choose two that are sufficiently different. Note that a question could ask you to compare two specified approaches, unlike this question which allows you to choose. There are 2 marks for clarity and communication and 2 marks for balance and breadth. This leaves 4 AO1 marks and 4 AO2 marks. Describing two approaches would get the AO1 marks, as long as the descriptive points lead to a comparison point. The comparison points (in what ways the two chosen approaches are similar and/or different) would earn the AO2 marks.

(5) To earn all 6 marks, you could either give three developments and briefly outline each or you could give two and describe them in more detail.

(6) This question is the same style as question 3, but is worth 12 and not 14 marks. There are 2 marks for clarity and communication and 2 marks for balance and breadth, which leaves 4 AO1 marks and 4 AO2 marks. Description of the humanistic approach to therapies is required for the AO1 marks, and evaluation and comment for the AO2 marks. This evaluation can include some reference to other approaches, but remember that this will not gain many marks — you must focus on the approach that is asked for.

Answers

(1) Flooding is a behavioural technique used to help overcome phobias. ✓ People are immersed in their fear and their anxiety levels then rise considerably. Anxiety levels can only rise to a certain extent before the energy needed to maintain them must run out, so the anxiety level should fall. ✓ As the exposure to the feared object continues, the individuals should feel less anxious, and then should interpret that as being cured of their phobia. ✓ The idea rests on principles of classical conditioning. The original situation is that the object gives a fear response and the final situation should be that the feared object gives a relaxed response. ✓

> 🖉 There is enough here for full marks. The first mark is given for the treatment itself and the remaining 3 marks are given for describing it. Although the links to classical conditioning do not add much to the description, the final sentence helps to show what is done in flooding. An example, such as when Wolpe drove a girl round in a car to cure her of a phobia about cars, would have added to the answer, but an example is only likely to gain 1 mark.

(2) The main problem with flooding is that it is very unethical and involves a great deal of anxiety. ✓ It cannot be used to treat some disorders either because it is based on classical conditioning principles, so it relates only to reflexive responses like fear. ✓

> 🖉 This answer scores 2 out of 4 marks. It gives an ethical point and a point about limitation of the therapy. The explanation of its limitation is reasonable and almost earns 2 marks. More marks could have been gained by examining alternative therapies for phobias, such as systematic desensitisation, which can be said to be more successful and more often used. The choice of therapy varies between therapists. There are those who would claim that flooding is no longer used, and those who would claim that systematic desensitisation is no longer used, so it is hard to be precise in this area. These issues can, however, be raised and examined.

(3) The medical/biological approach treats mental disorders as illnesses that have a biological cause and need biological treatments to cure them. ✓(AO1) The approach involves underlying genetic and biochemical factors, such as problems with the balance of neurotransmitters. ✓(AO1) It could be that there is brain damage or that brain differences are causing the problem. ✓(AO1) All these are physiological factors. One example of using the biological approach to look at disorders is looking at depression, which is said to be caused by imbalance in neurotransmitters, and treatment is by drugs which change the neurotransmitter patterns. ✓ ✓(AO1) A problem with this is that depression could be caused by social factors, and stress brought about by social situations. ✓(AO2) Other mental disorders have been said to have psychological explanations, such as the psychodynamic explanation for eating disorders. ✓(AO2) In addition, there could be biological problems in mental disorders, but it is hard to see whether these problems cause the disorder or are there because of the disorder. ✓(AO2) Just because drug treatment works does not mean that there is a biological cause. ✓(AO2) On the other hand, one good thing about biological explanations is that the evidence is often quite solid, resting as it tends to do on scientific measures such as scans and EEG measures. ✓(AO2)

> 🅔 This answer scores 5 AO1 marks and 5 AO2 marks. It is a good, balanced answer, so 2 marks for balance and breadth are awarded, and the spelling, grammar and use of terminology are good, so 2 marks for clarity and communication are also added. It therefore gets full marks. Although 2 AO2 marks are given specifically for contrasting the medical approach with a social one, and for contrasting it with a psychodynamic one, this is the maximum that you would get for giving alternative explanations. These points are worth making, to show limitations with the approach discussed, but remember to focus on the approach asked for in the question rather than on any alternatives you mention.

(4) The behaviourist and the medical/biological approaches are both commonly used as treatments and therapies for mental disorders. The behaviourist approach focuses on mental disorders as involving maladaptive behaviour, and the idea is to change this behaviour to be more appropriate. ✓(AO1) The medical/biological approach focuses on mental disorders as being illnesses with biological causes that need to be treated by medical intervention. ✓(AO1) It can be seen, then, that behaviourist treatments are going to be different from medical ones. Medical treatments involve drugs or surgery, whereas behaviourist treatments involve those like systematic desensitisation. ✓(AO1) There are few similarities here; indeed, the treatments would be given for different disorders. Phobias can be successfully treated by conditioning the individual to relax with the feared object, rather than fear it. ✓(AO1) It might be possible for the person to take anti-anxiety drugs instead, but this is not likely to happen as phobias are specific fears. ✓(AO2) If, however, the person is suffering from generalised anxiety, where fears are not specific, then drugs might be useful at least in the short term. ✓(AO2) The two approaches are different because they are used to treat different disorders. They also differ because they see different causes for mental disorders and focus on different areas. ✓(AO2) In theory, they could be used in combination. For example, for systematic desensitisation to work the person must be able to relax successfully and perhaps drug treatment might help with this aspect. ✓(AO2)

> 🅔 This is a good essay which scores 2 marks for clarity and communication and 2 marks for balance and breadth. It also earns 4 marks each for AO1 and AO2 material. It is not easy to show where these marks are allocated as the answer tends to give description within evaluation. 3 AO1 marks are given for describing the two approaches and for then giving examples of therapies within them. 1 AO1 mark is given for expanding on the treatment of phobias. 2 AO2 marks are given for showing how two problems (phobias and generalised anxiety) might be treated differently and successfully by each of the two approaches. A further AO2 mark is given for emphasising how the two approaches are different in what they see as causes. The final AO2 mark is given for the suggestion that the approaches could work together. This shows that the candidate is thinking about the answer.

(5) Recent developments in dealing with mental disorders take into account the social factors involved. For example, the diathesis–stress model suggests that social pressures and stressors can have a role in the development of disorders such as schizophrenia and depression. One development has been to try to stop disorders from developing in the first place, and drop-in centres have developed. ✓ The idea is that if there is somewhere for someone to get advice and help before stress builds up so much that a full disorder develops, then this is prevention. ✓ The aim is to provide 24-hour cover, but this is difficult in practice, and telephone advice is often part of the cover. ✓ Another development is care in the community. The idea is that people become institutionalised and part of the problem can then be the difficulty of reintegrating them into the community. ✓ Half-way houses and day hospitals are used to help people to live in their own communities and families, but still have the support they need. ✓

> 🖉 This answer gives a good introduction but does not actually describe developments straight away. However, it goes on to describe two elements: drop-in centres and care in the community. In both cases, there is elaboration to say what these are, earning 2 marks for each. The third mark for 'drop-in centres' is given partly for the reference to telephone advice and partly for introducing the role of stressors and the implied need for prevention. The description of community care is not quite enough to earn 3 marks, so 5 marks are given in total. The final mark could have come from giving another example, such as the growth of counselling organised through GPs.

(6) The humanistic approach to mental disorders takes a different view from many of the others. Other approaches, such as the medical/biological one, tend to look at mental disorders as illnesses that must be cured. The humanistic approach focuses on mental health rather than mental illness. ✓(AO2) It holds that we all have the drive to self-actualise and to reach our potential. This is our goal. ✓(AO1) If we are prevented somehow from being able to realise our full potential (to self-actualise), then this might mean we do not achieve mental health. ✓(AO1) Rather than focusing on illness, humanists focus on how everyone can achieve mental health, and they suggest therapies such as client-centred therapy to enable self-actualisation to take place. ✓(AO1) The idea is to give people unconditional positive regard and to empathise with them, to allow them the space to find out what they are aiming for (in order to self-actualise). ✓(AO1) The problem is that it is not easy to give everyone unconditional positive regard or to empathise with everyone. Another problem with the humanistic approach is that it denies that any biological problem can lead to a disorder. For the humanist, schizophrenia would come from problems with living. When considering some people with schizophrenia, for example those with catatonic schizophrenia or with very disorganised thinking and speech patterns, it is hard to see how this is the result of not self-actualising and it is hard to see how just listening could help. ✓ ✓(AO2)

> 🖉 This answer is focused and gives a lot of information. The answer is written clearly, so 2 marks for clarity and communication are given. The humanistic approach is

described and evaluated, with a good balance of description and argument, so 2 marks for balance and breadth are given. There are 4 AO1 marks and 3 AO2 marks, so the answer almost gains full marks. The point about the problems in empathising could earn another AO2 mark, but needs expanding further for the mark to be given.

Section 3

Specific mental disorders

(1) Describe the main features/symptoms of *one* of the mental disorders you have studied. (3 marks, AO1)

(2) Outline *one psychological* factor which may be a possible cause of the disorder you described in question 1. (3 marks, AO1)

(3) Evaluate that factor as a possible cause of the disorder you described in question 1. (6 marks, AO2)

(4) Name *one* mental disorder you have studied for clinical psychology. (Choose a different disorder from the one you used in question 1.) (1 mark, AO1)

(5) Describe the main features of the disorder you named in question 4. (4 marks, AO1)

(6) Evaluate the possible role of *physiological* factors in causing the disorder you named in question 4. (5 marks, AO2)

(7) Evaluate the possible role of *social* factors in causing the disorder you named in question 4. (5 marks, AO2)

(8) Discuss the role of *psychological* factors in explaining *two* mental disorders that you have studied. (16 marks, essay)

(1) If you are asked for features and/or symptoms of a mental disorder, as in this question, you can use any detail to describe it. For example, a symptom of schizophrenia is thought disturbances, and a feature is that approximately 1% of any population is likely to be diagnosed with it. If you are asked only for symptoms, don't include this latter point. Note that eating disorders, anxiety disorders and mood disorders are not 'one' disorder, they are types of disorder. In these cases, choose either bulimia or anorexia, either unipolar or bipolar depression and so on. 1 mark is for naming the mental disorder and 2 further marks are for describing it.

(2) Note that 'one' and 'psychological' are both in italics. This is because you should have studied physiological and social factors as well, but here you must choose a psychological factor. You need to focus on one factor only, and not give an outline of more than one. If you do give more than one, they will all be marked and the one gaining most marks will gain credit. Always read the question carefully to make sure that you answer it correctly. Psychodynamic explanations are useful as they are psychological, as are cognitive explanations. Explanations such as labelling tend to be called social even though there is an element of psychology to them. Remember to keep to the disorder you chose in question 1. It might be hard to limit your answer to a particular disorder (e.g. bipolar or unipolar disorders), so you may find you need to talk about mood disorders in general. For this part of the question, that is usually acceptable, as explanations do not always differentiate between the two (the same applies to eating disorders). 1 mark is for the factor, and 2 more marks are for elaborating on it.

(3) Again you must refer to the disorder (or type of disorder) you used for question 1. You must refer to the factor you gave in question 2 as well. You need to make evaluative points. You could give six separate points, or three points elaborated slightly, or two points elaborated well. One way of evaluating a factor is to contrast it with another (for example, saying the psychological factor you chose does not take into account physiological factors). Although this is a good idea, it would not earn many marks. 1 mark might be awarded for giving an alternative, but no further marks would be awarded for describing that factor as you should be evaluating the one you are focusing upon.

(4) There are four types of mental disorder listed in the specification, and there are specific disorders within these types. Name one of these specific disorders. Questions 4 to 7 would make one whole question on the exam paper, so note that later you have to evaluate physiological and social factors and their role in this disorder. You should therefore pick a mental disorder where you know something about these factors. You also need to be able to describe the symptoms.

(5) Give the main symptoms of the disorder you chose for question 4 above. What would a person suffering from it experience? Other features, such as which gender is most likely to experience this disorder, are valid too. You need to make four clear points or expand upon two points, as 4 marks are available.

(6) Keeping to the same disorder, examine how useful physiological explanations for it are. You can say very briefly what physiological explanations do not do, but don't get sidetracked. For 5 marks, you can either give five different points, or expand upon two or three different points.

(7) This is similar to question 6 above, but this time you need to focus on social explanations. The same comments apply. Be sure to write enough to gain 5 marks.

(8) This is an essay question, with 2 marks for clarity and communication and 2 marks for balance and breadth. You need to demonstrate good grammar, spelling and correct use of terms for the clarity and communication marks. You must answer the question well for the balance and breadth marks, for example focusing clearly on two mental disorders and, in both cases, describing and commenting on the role of psychological factors. Note the similarity in the terms 'psychological' and 'physiological'. It is very easy to misread these in an examination, so pay particular attention to them. There are 6 AO1 marks and 6 AO2 marks. As there are two mental disorders, consider each to have 3 AO1 and 3 AO2 marks. To earn these you need to describe psychological factors that may have a role in the disorder (enough for 3 marks) and then evaluate those factors (enough for 3 marks). Then do the same for the other disorder.

■ ■ ■

Answers

(1) Symptoms of schizophrenia include auditory hallucinations, maladaptive thinking and maladaptive behaviour. ✓✓ Maladaptive thinking could be talking about one thing and then going off into another subject, while maladaptive behaviour could be rocking or holding a specific pose for a long time. ✓

> *e* This is a reasonably good answer. 1 mark is given for the group of symptoms in the first sentence and 1 mark for the mental disorder itself. Then a further mark is given for the elaboration. This answer does get full marks, but there is much more that could be said about thought disturbances or types of schizophrenia and it is advisable to give a little more detail than is included in this answer to be on the safe side.

(2) Growing up in a schizophrenogenic family is believed to be a psychological factor that causes schizophrenia. ✓ Perhaps a sufferer was not provided with uncondi-tional love and was not brought up in a loving and caring environment.

> *e* This answer uses good terminology, and earns 1 mark for the idea of a schizo-phrenogenic family, which is a psychological factor. The explanation, however, is not good. More should be said about the conflicting demands a schizophrenogenic family can make, and mention should be made of the confused communications.

(3) The psychological factor outlined above does take into account social factors in the development of schizophrenia, but does not look at genetic factors. ✓ Tests were done on monozygotic twins and showed that if one twin had schizophrenia, the other one had approximately a 50% chance of developing schizophrenia too. DZ twins, however, showed a much lower concordance rate, which suggests a genetic cause for schizophrenia. Another biochemical explanation is the dopamine hypothesis, which suggests that excess dopamine causes schizophrenia. ✓ The social and biological factors can be brought together in the diathesis–stress expla-nation, which suggests a genetic predisposition perhaps, and then social triggers.

> *e* This answer contains some good psychology but does not answer the question well. 1 mark can be given for contrasting the schizophrenogenic family explanation with a genetic one, and another mark for saying neurotransmitters could be a cause. However, although mentioning the diathesis–stress model could also be made useful, it is not related here to the schizophrenogenic family. In fact, in this answer it is not at all clear that the candidate understands the idea of a schizophrenogenic family. More could be said about the problem that schizophrenics may seem to come from a family with confused communication patterns, but that these patterns could be as much due to having someone in the family with schizophrenia as being a cause of the illness. Evidence for such a family existing, and having a family member with schizo-phrenia, could be given too. This answer scores 2 marks out of 6.

(4) Schizophrenia.

e This is correct, for **1** mark. Other possible answers include bipolar or unipolar disorder, bulimia, anorexia, phobias.

(5) Schizophrenia appears in around 1% of the population. There are different types of schizophrenia, including catatonic schizophrenia where the individual might stay in one pose for a very long time. ✓ Those with schizophrenia tend to have disorganised thoughts, and can suffer from delusions and hallucinations. ✓ There are positive symptoms, such as paranoid thoughts, in that these are what a schizophrenic has that others (normal people) do not. ✓ Negative symptoms, such as flat affect (no emotions), are symptoms that those with schizophrenia do not have but others (normal people) do. ✓

e This answer earns all **4** marks as it outlines some of the symptoms well.

(6) Schizophrenia is thought to be genetic. Studies of MZ twins, who share 100% of their genes, show that they are quite a lot more likely both to suffer from schizophrenia than DZ twins, who share 50% of their genes like any other pair of siblings. These studies come up with different concordance rates for MZ twins, but the rate tends to be around 50%. However, although it seems that genes have a role in the development of schizophrenia, if only genes were responsible we would expect there to be a 100% concordance rate in MZ twins, and this is by no means the case. ✓✓ There could be a genetic predisposition for it. Others have looked at brain structure and claimed that differences such as size of ventricles are connected with schizophrenia. However, not all those with schizophrenia have enlarged ventricles, and also it is hard to see whether such brain differences cause the illness or are caused by it. ✓✓ The dopamine hypothesis suggests that schizophrenia is a result of excess dopamine. As anti-schizophrenic drugs tend to work by blocking this excess, this is evidence for the dopamine hypothesis. However, again it could be that the schizophrenia causes the excess dopamine and not the other way around. ✓

e This is a thorough answer. First, a physiological factor is outlined and then evaluated, which earns **2** marks. The description of the factor in itself does not get the marks, as the question asks for the role of such factors to be *evaluated*. However, when description is followed by an evaluation, then the material is credited. The same applies to the second suggestion that brain differences are involved — this point gets a double mark when the evaluation is given. The third point could well be worth **2** marks on the same principle, but only **5** marks are available.

(7) It is possible that having a schizophrenogenic mother causes schizophrenia. Communication patterns between the individual and such a mother might lead to confusion, which leads to schizophrenia. Some families with schizophrenic members do seem to have confused communication patterns, but this might be due to having the disorder in the family, as much as being a cause of the problem.

e Unfortunately, this answer does not focus on a social factor, and no marks are gained. Saying that schizophrenia (perhaps reactive schizophrenia) arises from stressful situations and that a social stressor can trigger the disorder would be more appropriate. To evaluate this, it would be useful to consider the diathesis–stress model and to suggest that the stressor might trigger a certain type of schizophrenia, but is not likely to cause all types of schizophrenia. You could expand upon this argument for the 5 marks or give a labelling explanation for schizophrenia.

(8) Psychological factors are often considered to have a role in mental disorders. They may not be seen as the whole cause, but can be seen as contributory. One example is the idea that schizophrenia is caused by poor communication patterns in the family, especially on the part of the mother. ✓(AO1) This form of mother is called the schizophrenogenic mother. The idea is that a mother might cause a double-bind situation. On one hand, children are asked to give love in the form of a hug, for example, and on the other hand when they go to give a hug they may be pushed away. They are in a double-bind situation and cannot understand how to behave. ✓✓(AO1) This can cause problems such as schizophrenia. A problem with this explanation is that this sort of mother is not found in all cases — although such poor communication patterns are found in some families where there is a schizophrenic. ✓(AO2) It has been claimed that the family problems are as likely to be a result of having a family member with the mental disorder as to have caused the mental disorder. ✓(AO2) Another mental disorder where psychological factors are said to have a role is unipolar disorder. Depression can be triggered by stressors and reactive depression can be triggered by events such as a bereavement or divorce. ✓(AO1) One reason why depression might continue long enough after such events to warrant treatment is that psychological factors, such as negative thinking patterns and low self-esteem, can prolong feelings of worthlessness that characterise depression. ✓✓(AO1) These factors can be treated by cognitive therapies and these can be successful, which is evidence that psychological factors might cause depression. ✓(AO2) However, other explanations for depression include the role of serotonin, and drug treatment involving serotonin, for example, can help to alleviate the symptoms — which seems to suggest that there might be a physiological cause for depression rather than a psychological one. ✓(AO2)

e This answer is balanced and well written. Two disorders are dealt with, as asked for, and psychological factors are focused upon. 2 balance and breadth marks and 2 clarity and communication marks are given. For the first disorder, schizophrenia, there is a clear psychological 'explanation' that earns all 3 AO1 marks. The explanation is given and then expanded upon with good use of terms. Then there is some evaluation: first, saying that this may not explain all schizophrenia, although there is some evidence; second, that it could be the illness that causes the family problems. Another point is needed for the third AO2 mark. The second sentence could have been expanded upon for another mark, or a comment about method could have been made, such as the reliance on retrospective data — data about family communication patterns tend to be gathered after the person has been diagnosed. For the second disorder, the 3 AO1 marks are given. The answer looks at stressors and expands to consider types of stressor (e.g. bereavement and divorce) and responses (e.g. low self-esteem, feelings of worthlessness and negative thinking patterns). However, only 2 of the AO2 marks are given. 1 mark is for saying that cognitive therapy seems to work, and this is evidence, and the other is for saying that levels of serotonin are implicated in depression too, and this could be an alternative explanation. The final AO2 mark could have been gained by discussing other factors in developing depression, such as whether there is a social network. Those with a social network are less likely to develop the same level of negative feelings, so it seems that social and psychological factors are all at work.